Danielle

Some People
Make Headlines
While Others
Make History

10/16/15

Edward E. McGill

FOR THE
LOVE OF LIFE

LOVE

HOPE   FAITH

Transition from
Darkness to Light

GOD

EDWARD E. MCGILL

Order this book online at www.trafford.com
or email orders@trafford.com

Most Trafford titles are also available at major online book retailers.

Printed in the United States of America.

ISBN: 978-1-4669-0772-0 (sc)
ISBN: 978-1-4669-0774-4 (hc)
ISBN: 978-1-4669-0773-7 (e)

Library of Congress Control Number: 2011962474

Trafford rev. 03/17/2014

 www.trafford.com

North America & international
toll-free: 1 888 232 4444 (USA & Canada)
fax: 812 355 4082

CONTENTS

Dedications

Above and beyond I have come to recognize that my writing has been delivered to me as a God given gift.

Therefore it is only by right that it should be given back to God first and then to those who supported me along with my love ones as well.

Love goes beyond what anyone could ever imagine and it comes to a point where you know longer believe.

You know!

I would like to thank all of those who stood by my side, and encouraged me to continue writing. I would like to thank God for allowing me to go through the things that I needed to go through in order to be the man that I am today. I truly feel that I have been greatly blessed for that I dedicate this book to all of my readers with great hopes that it embraces whatever inspiration that may be upon you. I also dedicate this book to my mother, brother and sisters, my children and, my dearly beloved wife whom inspired me to publish my materials instead of collecting dust in the attic. She has shown me an unconditional love that I will never turn my back on and for that I plan to spend the rest of my life with her. Kathy A. McGill, I love you. Also for the readers I truly hope that my inspiration finds you and your families in all good health mentally, physically, and of course spiritually. Let all continue to be well under God's umbrella of peace and blessings.

For The Love of Life

Just a few lines to all my readers as you get deeper into this book you may find that there is more company around than just you and I. The gift that has been given to me is a blessing for which I deeply respect. A spirit of greatness has designed an art of poetry deep down within me and also provided me with the capability to express different views of inspiration and emotions from others. Everything that you read is given from the heart and personal experiences so as you begin to read be at ease and comfortable as I relax your mind, body, and soul. You may also find at some point somewhere in this book a void in your life may be fulfilled and for all that it means I am only a messenger for the one and only true author, the spirit above.

An endless journey of searching for love

Peace Be With You All

For The Love of Life

It's a fascinating thing
To know what it means
To look at it for what it's worth
And not what it seems.
Deep in the heart
There's a richness to find
Its nourishment flows
Through the body, soul and mind
As love offers itself
A creation begins to unfold
An inspirational embrace
That will protect and hold
As a rainbow of tears
Stretches across the sky
It's the reflection of the truth
From the peaceful faces that cry
For the love of life
I will give my heart to try
For the love of life
I will give my heart, and also die.

FOR THE LOVE OF LIFE

BY EDWARD E. MCGILL
POETRY
FOR THE MIND, BODY,
AND SOUL

TYPES OF LITERATURE
SPIRITUAL
ROMANCE
FRIENDSHIP
BIRTHDAYS
WEDDING VOWS
SPRING MOMENTS
WINTER MOMENTS
BABY SHOWERS
ANYTHING PERTAINING TO LOVE AND
LIFE!
THIS POETRY IS WRITTEN ESPECIALLY
TO BRING THE LOVE BACK

1)
MY LIFE

I WRITE OUT OF INSPIRATION
I BELIEVE IN KEEPING IT REAL
I SEARCH FOR THAT DESTINY
THAT NO PRICE CAN FULFILL
OUT OF ALL THE SACRAFICIES
TO GIVE AND TAKE
I REALIZE IT'S MY LIFE
HEAVEN AND HELL I MAKE
I'VE LEARNED TO COMPROMISE
WITH THE REASON TO DECIDE
WHICH ROAD I WILL TAKE
FOR A SMOOTH OR BUMPY RIDE
I BELIEVE IN HINDEN TALENTS
THE SECRET WAY TO BLEND
BECAUSE THERES A BEND IN THE ROAD
DOESN'T MEAN IT'S THE END
I BELIEVE IT'S POSSIBLE
FOR ANYBODY TO WIN
THE CHOICE IS REVEALED
THROUGH RIGHTOUSNESS OR SIN
THE KEY TO LIFE
IS TO BE GOOD TO YOURSELF
MIND, BODY AND SOUL
CARESSING YOUR HEALTH
ALWAYS LOOK FORWARD TO GAIN
FOR IN THIS YOU WILL REMAIN

2)
THE CONFESSION

I SHARE WITH YOU A DEEPNESS
I KNOW THAT YOU WILL FEEL
THE IMPRESSIONS IN MY LIFE
FROM THE HEART, AND TRULY REAL
I USE TO WEAR A MASK
TO PRETEND THAT THINGS WERE ALRIGHT
BUT DEEP DOWN IN MY HEART
I WAS MISSERABLE AND UPTIGHT
EVERY WHERE I REACHED OUT
I FOUND TO BE NOTHING THERE
LIFE TURNED ITS BACK ON ME
AND EVERYTHING SEEMED UNFAIR
FEELING STRIPPED OF MY SOUL
MY HEART DEEPLY AT A LOSS
TO REGAIN MY TRUE SELF AGAIN
O'HOW MUCH WOULD IT COST
SHEDDING TEARS OF SUFFERING PAIN
FOR ALL RIGHTOUSNESS I TRULY CRAVED
HOPING SOMEONE WAS LISTENING TO ME
IN THE DEEPEST NEED TO BE SAVED
AS I DROPPED TO MY KNEES
I HEARD A TRIMBLING VOICE
SAYING BE STRONG MAN
YOU STILL HAVE A CHOICE
I RAISED MY HEAD IN FEAR
AS TEARS RAN FROM MY EYES
ONCE AGAIN THE VOICE SAID TO ME
DO AWAY WITH YOUR FALSE DISGUISE

FOR I HAVE MADE YOUR LIFE A NEW
PROMISE TO KEEP IT RIGHTOUS
AND ETERNAL LIFE I WILL GIVE TO YOU
I HAVE GIVEN YOU THE LIGHT
FOR NOW YOU ARE MINE
WHENEVER YOU'RE IN TROUBLE
JUST CALL ANYTIME
YOU HAVE PAID THE PRICE
AND NOW YOU ARE FREE
I GRANT YOU THIS GIFT
BY THE POWER INVESTED IN ME
FOLLOW MY INSTRUCTIONS
REMEMBER THE PLACE
WHERE YOU LEFT DISTRUCTION
AND RECIEVED GRACE.

3)
THE WITNESS

THERE'S A WITNESS IN THE CLOUDS
WHOSE PROMISE IS TO RELIEVE
THOSE WHO HAVE FAITH
THOSE WHO BELIEVE
THERE'S A WITNESS IN THE CLOUDS
WHO PROVIDES FOR OUR EVERY NEED
WHO SHOWS US GREAT LOVE
EVERY RACE, COLOR AND CREED
THERE'S A WITNESS IN THE CLOUDS
WHOSE LOVE I LONG TO KEEP
OF POWERFUL SPIRITUAL VALUE
SO TRUE, SO DEEP
THERE'S A WITNESS IN THE CLOUDS
WHO OFFERS US SALVATION
AND GIVES US THE POWER
TO OVERCOME TEMPTATION
THERE'S A WITNESS IN THE CLOUDS
WHOSE GUIDANCE IS BY LIGHT
WHOSE PROTECTION IS LAW
TO KEEP US ALL WITHIN RIGHT
TO KNOW THIS WITNESS
IS TO ONLY BE FREE
I STATE THIS AS A FACT
BECAUSE HE LIVES IN ME

4)
THE LOSS OF A LOVE ONE

ALTHOUGH WE MAY FEEL A SADNESS
OF LOOSING SOMEONE DEAR
WE CAN STILL CHERISH THE MEMORIES
OF THE SPIRIT THAT STILL LIES NEAR
AS LIFE CONTINUES TO UNFOLD
WE'RE GIVEN THE STRENGTH TO SUSTAIN
THROUGH TRIALS AND TRIBULATIONS
FOR THE PRAISING OF FAITH STILL REMAIN
WE ARE THE MAKERS AND THE MASTERS
OF OUR OWN DESTINY
FOR THE LIFE THAT WE SO MISS
HAS FINALLY BEEN SET FREE
TO BE JOINED WITH OUR HEAVENLY FATHER
WHO DESIGNED THE UNIVERSITY
AND PREPARED A PLACE
WHERE THERE IS NO ADVERSITY
SO LET IT BE AS A MEMORY
THAT DEATH IS NO ENEMY TO MAN
FOR THE SOUL IS RESTING IN PEACE
SECURE BY GODS RIGHT HAND.

5)
IT'S NO MYSTERY

THERE IS NO ACCIDENT
FOR THE WAY MY LIFE HAS CHANGED
THE AUTHOR OF ALL CREATION
HOLDS THE LAW AND THE POWER TO ARRANGE
THERE WERE TIMES WHEN I'VE CRIED
FOR SOMEONES HELP I'VE CRAVED
AFRAID OF WHAT WAS IN STORE FOR ME
NEEDING TO BE SAVED
THIS IS JUST THE BEGINNING
FOR THE BATTLE HAS TAKEN FLIGHT
TO PURIFY MY SOULS DIRECTION
WITH SALVATION AS MY LIGHT
I WITH-HOLD THE TRUE HONORS
TO SAY NOW I'M FINALLY FREE
NEVER TO BE IN DOUBT
IN THE FAITH OF WHAT I BELIEVE
TO BE AWARE IS TO BE ALIVE
FOR HIS SPIRIT OFFERS A LOT
AND TIME NEVER WAS
WHEN MAN WAS NOT

6)
HE'S A GOOD MAN

AS A BABY WE ARE BORN INNOCENT
HAVING TO CRAWL BEFORE WE WALK
ALSO BLOWING BUBBLES
BEFORE LEARNING TO TALK
THE STRENGTH AND GROWING OF CURIOSITY
IS A WHOLE NEW PROGRAM
BEGINNING WITH PLEASE AND THANK YOU
YES SIR AND YES MAM
EDUCATION IS MANDATORY
SELF RESPECT WILL BE THE KEY
FOR THE EYES OF THE LORD
THE GLORYFUL AND RIGHTOUSNESS YOU WILL SEE
FOLLOW THE LAWS OF COMMANDMENT
IS TO HONOR AND OBEY
HIS BLESSINGS WILL COME UPON YOU
IN THE MOST BEAUTIFUL WAY
JUST ASK FOR FORGIVENESS
YOUR SOUL WILL NEVER DIE
GOD KEEPS HIS PROMISES
HE WILL NEVER LIE
THY SHALL KNEEL DOWN AND PRAY
RAISE A HAND IN THE AIR
HIS LOVE AND FORGIVENESS
IS TO JUDGE EVERYONE FAIR

7)
HOPE AND BELIEVE

BROKE DOWN LIKE A SHOTGUN
I'M AT THE END OF MY ROPE
BUT IT'S THE FAITH OF WHOM I BELIEVE IN
THAT KEEPS GIVING ME HOPE
GROWING STRONGER DAY BY DAY
I'VE LEARNED NOT TO BE AFRAID
AND I WILL ALWAYS REMEMBER
THE TRICKS OF THE TRADE
GIFTED WITH THE TALENT TO LIGHTEN ANY ROOM
SOMEDAY I'LL MAKE SOMEONE HAPPY
AND BECOME THE PROMISED GROOM
LIFTED WTH THE HEAVENLY SPIRIT
THAT KEEPS MY WHOLE LIFE ALIVE
FOR IT'S MY PESONALITY AND CHARCTER
WHICH WILL NEVER DIE
I HAVE ONE CHANCE LEFT TO FULFILL MY HEART
CAUSE I'VE NEVER BELIEVED IN
IT'S TOO LATE TO START
MY EYES ARE OPEN WIDE
READY TO LIVE THE LIFE THAT IS RIGHT
AND FOR THE REST OF MY DAYS
I'LL SPEND STANDING IN THE LIGHT

8)
I WANT TO BE SOMEBODY

I WANT TO BE SOMEBODY
MORE THAN JUST A BODY WITH A NAME
I WANT TO BE IN THE MIST
OF LIGHT FORTURNE AND FAME
I WANT TO RIDE THE CLOUDS
IN SEARCH OF MY DESTINY
I WANT TO SHARE THE GIFTS
AND THE BLESSINGS GIVEN TO ME
I WANT TO GIVE MY HEART
FOR CARING AND HELPING OTHERS
I WANT TO SHARE MY LOVE
WITH MY SISTERS AND BROTHERS
I WANT TO GIVE MY LIFE
FOR I HAVE A PURPOSE TO DEFINE
I WANT TO SHARE WITH THE WORLD
AND CLAIM WHAT IS MINE
I WANT TO BE SOMEBODY
MANY NIGHTS I LAY BACK AND CRY
I WANT TO BE SOMEBODY
BECAUSE STARS BELONG IN THE SKY

9)
SUCCESS

SUCCESS IS A TALENT
THAT GROWS FROM THE HEART TO THE MIND
IT'S THE STRENGTH OF DETERMINATION
FOR A PURPOSE TO DEFINE
IT'S THE STRONGEST EFFORT TO LEARN
THE WILL TO WANT TO GROW
TO RECOGNIZE YOUR ABILITIES
ARE THE WAYS TO LET IT FLOW
SUCCESS IS A HONEST MISSION
OF HARD WORK AND DEDICATION
IT'S THE STRENGTH OF WHAT YOU LOVE
AND THE RESPECT OF APPRECIATION
THE FUTURE HOLDS NO PROMISES
BUT THE BLESSINGS ARE IN THE LIGHT
ONLY TO BELHOLD YOUR DESTINY
NEVER GIVE UP THE FIGHT
SELF-ESTEEM IS THE MOTIVE
EDUCATION IS THE KEY
FOR THE SKY IS THE LIMIT
TO ALL THE GLORY YOU'LL SEE
IT'S WRITTEN IN THE BOOK OF WISDOM
SEALED WITH A LINEN
THAT SUCCESS IS YOUR DESTINY
AND YOUR FUTURE IS SHINNING

10)
MY MARRIAGE VOWS
THE GOLDEN SEAL

THESE VOWS I DEDICATE TO YOU
TO HONOR WITH LOYALTY
AND A FAITH THAT IS ALSO TRUE
I PROMISE TO LOVE AND CHARISH YOU
UNTIL DEATH DO US APART
I GIVE YOU THE BEST YEARS OF MY LIFE
ALL OF MY HEART
I PROMISE A TRUE VALUE OF DEVOTION
THAT WILL NEVER BREAK OR BEND
I WILL LOVE YOU TO THE FULLEST
AS MY WIFE AND BEST FRIEND
I PROMISE YOU MIND, BODY AND SOUL
OUR DESTINY WE WILL REACH
FOR ALL THE THINGS TO BEHOLD
AND THE SPIRIT TO TEACH
I PROMISE TO CARESS
FOR YOUR MOST SENSITIVE DESIRE
TO WARM YOU WHEN YOU'RE COLD
WITH AN EVERLASTING FIRE
I PROMISE TO GIVE YOU A LOVE
THAT IS TRIMMED IN GOLD
A LOVE THAT IS RICH
AND WILL NEVER GROW OLD
THANK YOU MY LOVE
FOR THIS NATURAL HIGH
I GIVE YOU MY HEART
UNTIL THE DAY I DIE

11)
MY ROSE

TIS A ROSE FOR A QUEEN
WHOSE BEAUTY I ADORE
BUT ONLY ONE ROSE TO SYMBOLIZE MY LOVE
I ONLY WISH I COULD GIVE YOU MORE
WE HAVE ESTABLISHED BETWEEN US
A BRIDGE OF COMMUNICATION
AND MY WORK ON THIS ROSE
IS WORK OF EXPRESSING JUST APPRECIATION
IN CASE NO ONE HAS TOLD YOU BEFORE
WHAT JOY TO LIFE YOU CAN BRING
THAT KNOWING A QUEEN LIKE YOU
MAKE ME FEEL LIKE A KING
I SAY THESE WORDS
AFTER CAREFULL CONSIDERATION
FOR I REALIZE THAT IN YOU
IS MY JOY, MY LIFE, MY EVERY INSPIRATION
I DON'T SAY THESE WORDS JUST TO FLATTER YOU
I'M SIMPLY SAYING WHAT I TRULY FEEL
AND WHEN YOU READ THEM KNOW IN HEART
THAT WITH YOU I'LL ALWAYS BE FOR REAL
SO UNTIL NEXT TIME
THESE VERSES I CLOSE
AND NO MATTER WHAT FATE I MAY FACE
YOU'LL ALWAYS BE MY ROSE

12)
MY ANGEL

I ONCE LOOKED UP TO THE HEAVENS
AIMLESSLY SEEKING MY DESTINY
THE CLOUDS WERE DARK AND UNYEILDING
AS THEY PASSED OVER ME
I CALLED OUT IN DESPIRATION
O'GOD WHAT IS MY DUE
HE SAID THE BEST IN MY CREATION
A SON I WILL GIVE TO YOU
I WANDERED AWAY IN TRIPDATION
AFRAID OF WHAT WAS IN STORE FOR ME
BUT THEN I MET A ANGEL OF SIMPLE MEANS
AND OF THE GREATEST NOBILITY
HER SMILE MY JOY
HER SADNESS MY PAIN
HER PRESSENCE IS MY SUNSHINE
AND HER TEARS MY RAIN
I SAY THESE WORDS WITH PRIDE AND JOY
ALL APPRECIATION THAT IS DUE
FOR I NOW KNOW MY DESTINY
IT'S WITH THE BEST IN ALL CREATION
AN ANGEL THAT'S YOU

13)
I FEEL YOU

WE'VE ALL BEEN THROUGH THE CHANGES
BY GAMES OF MANIPULATION
TO TAKE ONLY THE SAD ABUSE
OF FALSE FACES AND PERPETRATION
THE RESPECT FOR ANOTHERS LOVE
IS HONESTY WITHOUT ANY COST
TO BELIEVE WITH ALL SINCERITY
THAT ONE DAY THAT LOVE CAN BE LOST
LOVE IS A DEDICATIED EMOTION
OF WHAT THE HEART TRULY INSPIRES
THE STRENGTH OF COMMUNICATION
AND THE VALUES OF PRECIOUS DESIRES
WE CAN BRING OUT INNER FEELINGS
BY MEANS OF SHOWING CONCERN
SHARING LIFES EXPERICENCES TOGETHER
FOR UNDERSTANDING ALL WE CAN LEARN
TO CHARISH THE MOMENT OF PLEASURE
IS TO NOURISH THE FEELING IN HEART
NEVER TO BECOME A DISTANT
OF WHY OUR LOVE SHOULD EVER BE APART
IT'S ONLY IN MY HEART TO SAY
FOR I SPEAK ON THE THINGS THAT ARE TRUE
MY HEART IS PURE WITH SIMPLE OFFERINGS
THAT I WOULD LOVE TO SHARE WITH YOU

14)
CAN YOU FEEL ME

SOMETIMES WE SMILE
SOMETIMES WE CRY
FOR THAT GREAT FORTUNE
THAT LIES IN THE SKY
WITH EVERYTHING TO DESIRE
A DESTINY TO BEHOLD
THE INSPIRATION IN HEART
IS WORTH MORE THAN GOLD
TO FREE THE SPIRIT OF LOVE
FOR THE EYES TO TELL
THOSE WHO CAN'T SEE
CAN FEEL IT IN BRAIL
AN INSPIRATION SO DEEP
STIMULATING HEART AND MIND
TO CARESS THIS EMOTION
IS A POSESSION SO DEVINE
I SHARE WITH YOU MY DREAM
FOR YOU I LONG TO FEEL
TO BREATHE THE TRUE PASSION
OF A LOVE THAT IS REAL
I WANDER THROUGH THE NIGHT
FOLLOWING THE BRIGHTEST STAR
HOPING THAT IT WILL LEAD ME
TO WHERE EVER YOU ARE

15)
SOUL MATES

OUT OF ALL THE WORLDS PEOPLE
I FIND A BLESSING TO BELIEVE
THAT WE WERE BROUGHT TOGETHER
TO FULFILL A DESTINY
BEFORE OUR PHYSICAL FORMS
COULD WALK UPON THIS EARTH
OUR SPIRITUAL FORMS WERE DEVELOPED
FOR THE SAKE OF GIVING BIRTH
I CAN'T HELP BUT TO FEEL
THAT WE HAVE DONE THIS BEFORE
NOW WE HAVE BEEN BROUGHT TOGETHER
AS SOUL MATES TO DO IT ONCE MORE
FOR ALL THE LOVE AND HAPPINESS
THAT WE CAN OFFER TO ONE ANOTHER
WITH GOD AS OUR PROTECTOR
OUR BLANKET AND COVER
FOR ALL THAT CAN BE MEASURED
BY WHAT WE FEEL IS TRUE
THAT THERE ARE NO STRANGE HAPPENNINGS
WHY IT'S ME, AND YOU

16)
THIRSTY FOR YOU

LIKE THE SAP FROM A TREE
MY LOVE FOR YOU CONTINUES TO POUR
LIKE HONEY TO A BEE
I'M ALWAYS NEEDING YOU MORE
LIKE THE DESERT NEEDS WATER
TO COOL THE HOT SAND
MY HEART IS MELTING
FOR THE SOFT STROKE OF YOUR HAND
LIKE THE EARTH NEEDS MOTHER NATURE
TO MAKE THINGS GROW
I NEED YOUR LOVE
LET IT FLOW, LET IT FLOW
LIKE THE FLOWERS NEED SUNSHINE
TO MAKE COLORS O' SO BRIGHT
I NEED YOUR WISDOM
AND YOUR BEAUTIFUL INSIGHT
LIKE A KING NEEDS A QUEEN
TO BE HIS LOVING WIFE
YOU'RE THE WOMAN I'M FROZEN TO
FOR THE REST OF MY LIFE

17)
LAST NIGHT

LAST NIGHT I SAW THE SUNSET
IN YOUR DEEP BEAUTIFUL EYES
A HORIZON SO BEAUTIFUL
SO TENDER AND SO WISE
YOU'RE THE HIGH-LIGHT OF MY DREAMS
SO SEXY AND UNIQUE
IN SILENCE YOU SPEAK TO ME
THROUGH MY SYSTEM YOU CREEP
WHAT I SEE SO CLEARLY
IS A FACE SO BRIGHT
AND EYES THAT TWINKLE
LIKE THE STARS AT NIGHT
MY MOUTH BECOMES MOIST
IN DEEP NEED OF A KISS
FROM THE WOMAN I LOVE
LONG FOR AND MISS
WITH A FEELING OF SPECIALTY
TO BE TOGETHER AS ONE
I CAN'T WAIT UNTIL MORNING
TO LOOK IN YOUR EYES AND SEE THE SUN

18)
THE WALL OF CHARM

I WILL BUILD AROUND YOU
A WALL OF CHARM
A WALL OF SECURITY
I WILL LET NOTHING HARM
I WILL BUILD AROUND YOU
AN INSPIRATIONAL EMBRACE
THAT WILL TOUCH YOU NIGHT AND DAY
ANYTIME ANY PLACE
I WILL BUILD AROUND YOU
THE SWEET SONGS OF A DOVE
SHARING TEARS OF HAPPINESS
FROM THE FAUCET OF MY LOVE
I WILL BUILD AROUND YOU
A RIVER SO DEEP
OF ALL THE PRECIOUS THINGS
THAT YOU DREAM IN YOUR SLEEP
I WILL BUILD AROUND YOU
A WARM BURNING FIRE
THAT WILL LEAVE YOUR HEART MELTING
IN THE MIST OF OUR DESIRE

SWEET DREAMS

19)
SO CLOSE BUT YET SO FAR

GLIDING DEEP THROUGH THE NIGHT
LISTENING TO A QUIET STORM
THE THOUGHTS OF ONE SO BEAUTIFUL
TO BE CLOSE CARING AND WARM
IN THE MIST OF VISIONS
WHEN SILENCE CAN BE SO LOUD
THE LIGHT OF THE MOON
DISAPPEARS BEHIND A CLOUD
IF I ONLY HAD THE POWER
TO STEP INTO MY DREAMS
I COULD GIVE HER MY HEART
AND EVERYTHING THAT IT MEANS
FOR ALL IT COULD BE WORTH
MY FEELINGS TO TRULY ENHANCE
TO SHOW HER A REAL LOVE
SPOILING HER WITH ROMANCE
SOMEWHERE OUT THERE
SHE'S IS THE KEY TO MY LIFE
EVERYTHING I TRULY WANT
IN A WOMAN AND A WIFE
I PROPOSE TO YOU ON THIS DAY
WHERE EVER YOU MAY BE
A LIFE LONG COMMITMENT
IN THE LAND OF ETERNITY

20)
MIDNIGHT BLUE

SHE BECAME SO ALIVE
DEEP INTO MY DREAM
ALL I COULD DO
IS HOLD MY HEART AND SCREAM
SHE BROKE THROUGH THE BARRIERS
OF MY DEFENSE
TO HELP ME OVERCOME
THE PAIN OF PAST TENSE
SHE CREEPED INTO MY LIFE
WITHOUT A WISPER OR WARNING
THE BEAUTIFUL PART OF HER STYLE
IS HER SMILE IN THE MORNING
SHE IS MY HEART AND SOUL
WHO'S FOREVER ON MY MIND
SHE'S THE SPIRIT OF MY LIFE
I'LL NEVER LEAVE BEHIND
SHE'S THE FLAVOR OF MY DESIRE
SO TRULY COMPLETE
SHE'S THE SPICE OF CREATION
A FRUIT SO SWEET
FOR I'LL GIVE HER MY HEART
TO BE DEDICATED AND TRUE
SHE'S THE GIFT, AND A BLESSING
FROM OUT OF THE BLUE

21)
TOGETHER AT LAST

FINALLY OUT OF THE DARKNESS
I NOTICED A CERTAIN GLOW
THE FRAGRANCE OF INSCENTS
IN THE ATMOSPHERE IT FLOWS
CANDLES BURNING SOFTLY
MATCHING THE COLOR OF THE ROOM
CURTAINS CRACKED GENTLY
TO CATCH THE VIEW OF THE MOON
I SUDDENLY FELT YOUR TOUCH
THE SOFTNESS OF YOUR HANDS
WHAT THE NIGHT HOLDS IN STORE
IS WHAT OUR LOVE DEMANDS
YOU'VE GIVEN ME A FEELING
MY HEART YOU'VE CARRESSED
THE BEAUTIFUL WAY YOU PLEASE ME
LEAVES A PERMANENT ADDRESS
SOMETHING SPECIAL TO REMEMBER
ABOUT THE LOVE WE SHARE
IT'S THE GIFT OF ALL GIFTS
THAT WE CAN TAKE ANYWHERE
I SAY WITH ALL HONESTY
I CAN LET GO OF THE PAST
AND LOOK TOWARDS THE FUTURE
CAUSE WE ARE TOGETHER AT LAST

22)
SORROW

I CAN'T LIVE WITH IT ON MY CONSCIENCE
SO MANY THINGS I TRULY REGRET
I ONLY ASK FOR YOUR FORGIVENESS
BUT I KNOW IT'S HARD TO FORGET
ALL THE PITY AND MEMORIES OF WRONG
TO BE SORRY FOR EVERYTHING UNCLEAN
IF I ONLY KNEW IT BEFORE
A DIFFERENT LIGHT I WOULD HAVE SEEN
I IMPLY MY SENSE OF GUILT
AND THE TORTURING OF GRIEF I DREAD
I CAN HONESTLY SAY TO YOU NOW
THAT THE EVIL IN ME IS DEAD
I'M DEEPLY DISAPPOINTED IN MYSELF
OF BEING UNAWARE AND TRULY BLIND
I WILL GIVE ANYTHING TO THIS DAY
TO BE CLOSE TO YOUR HEART AND MIND
I KNOW THIS MAY COME AS A SURPRISE
BUT I REALIZE I'VE HURT A TRUE FRIEND
NEVER IN MY LIFE WILL I LIVE
TO SEE SUCH PAIN HAPPEN AGAIN
SO LET THIS BE NOTED AS A MEMORY
BEHIND THE HEARTS WE BREAK AND BEND
THAT OUR FRIENDSHIP IS TO BE LOVED
AND CHARISHED TO THE VERY END

23)
MY PRECIOUS PEARL

THERES NOT A DIAMOND IN THIS WORLD
THAT SHINES AS BEAUTIFUL AS YOU
FOR NO ONE CAN CARRY SUCH A LOVE
SO SINCERELY TRUE
SO INTOXICATING IS YOUR LOVE
MY HEART BURNS WITH TEARS OF FIRE
THE RICHNESS OF YOUR PEARL
IS MY SOULS DESIRE
MELTING WITH A DEEP LOVE
YOUR EVERY STROKE I ANTICIPATE
TO MAKE LOVE TO YOU
I CAN'T HARDLY WAIT
DROPS OF LOVE ROLL DOWN MY HEART
MY BODY BEGINS TO SWEAT
JUST IMAGINING YOU NAKED
SOFT SKIN, SO TENDER, AND WET
I CAN'T WAIT FOR THE DAY TO COME
MY LIFE WITH YOU I WILL NOT WASTE
CAUSE YOU'RE THE PEARL OF MY DREAMS
I SO DESPERATELY LOVE TO TASTE

24)
DRAMATIC LOVE

LOVE IS VERY POWERFUL
IT'S TASTE IS AS SWEET AS HONEY
IT'S VERY INTENSE
WHEN IT'S COMBINED WITH MONEY
SHE FLASHES LIKE JEWLERY
BRINGING TEMPTATION TO LUST
THE GAME OF PERPETRATION
BRINGS A HEART TO RUST
HER BODY IS SMOOTH AND SILKY
WITH A LIGHT GLAZE OF OIL
SHE WAITS IN A FINE NEGLIGEE
FOR YOUR HEART SHE WILL SPOIL
WITH A BOTTLE OF CHILLED CHAMPAGNE
TO PUT THE SITUATION AT EASE
NOW IT'S ONLY FOR A MOMENT
SHE WILL DROP TO HER KNEES
LAID BACK FOR THE PLEASURE
WITHOUT A WORRY IN THE WORLD
IT'S THE BEAUTY OF WHAT'S GOING ON
THAT MAKES YOU WONDER ABOUT THIS GIRL
SHE'S FEELING REAL LOVELY
A DREAM TO INSPIRE
DEEP IN YOUR HEART
SHE'S THE CURE OF YOUR DESIRE
BUT NOW COMES THE MOMENT
WHEN THE NOTE IS DUE
BECAUSE IN THE OTHER ROOM
ANOTHER WAITS TOO

25)
WHERE ARE YOU

I DON'T KNOW WHERE TO LOOK
I'VE SEARCHED NEAR AND FAR
I DON'T EVEN KNOW YOUR NAME
LET ALONE KNOW WHO YOU ARE
MY LIFE IS AT A MOMENT OF STILLNESS
HEALTHY BUT STILL UNFAIR
PATIENTLY WAITING FOR THE RARENESS
OF THE QUALITY OF LOVE AND CARE
ALTHOUGH I LIVE IN HUMBLENESS
MY LIFE IS STILL INCOMPLETE
TO BE WITHOUT TRUE LOVE
IS A CHALLENGE I HATE TO MEET
I CAN ONLY COUNT ON MY DREAMS
FOR THE FANTASIES REMAIN UNSPOKEN
MY HEART IS HELD WITH THE EMOTION
OF THE PAIN OF BEING NOT CHOSEN
I SAY IT WITH ALL SINCERITY
THAT I'LL NEVER GIVE UP ON LOVE
I OWE IT ALL TO THE HIGHEST SPIRIT
WHO HONORS THE HEAVENS ABOVE
I KNOW YOU'RE OUT THERE SOMEWHERE
TRUE LOVE ESPECIALLY FOR ME
TO ONLY BE IN MY PRESENCE
SET MY PAIN FREE

26)
WHO ARE YOU

MY DARLING,
WHY DO YOU DO THIS TO ME?
IN AND OUT OF MY DREAMS YOU GO
LEAVING ME IN SUSPENSE
YOUR NAME I DON'T EVEN KNOW
FAIR TO PARTLY CLOUDLY
I TRY TO VISULIZE YOUR FACE
IT'S THE WAY THAT YOU APPEAR
AND DISAPPEAR WITHOUT A TRACE
WEIGHING HEAVY ON MY MIND
YOUR TOUCH I LONG TO FEEL
SOMETIMES I WAKE UP CRYING
WISHING FOR IT TO BE REAL
I FEEL YOU ARE IN MY PRESENCE
I FEEL YOU IN MY SLEEP
FALLING INTO THAT DREAM
WHERE YOU ALWAYS SEEM TO CREEP
EACH TIME I REACH OUT FOR YOU
IT JUST DOESN'T SEEM FAIR
HOLDING OUT MY ARMS
FEELING NOTHING BUT AIR
I'VE FALLEN IN LOVE WITH YOU DEEPLY
I FEEL HOW PRESCIOUS YOU ARE
YOU'RE SPECIAL, A LOVE WORTH CHARISHING
SO CLOSE, BUT YET SO FAR

27)
HEART BEAT

MY HEART BEATS FOR YOU
I FEEL THE THINGS YOU SAY
YOU BRING ME MUCH HAPPINESS
BRIGHTEN MY DAY
I DON'T KNOW WHAT I WOULD DO
IF YOU WERE TO EVER LEAVE
I LOVE YOU SO SINCERELY
IN THIS I HOPE YOU BELIEVE
THINKING OF YOU EVERY DAY
DREAMING OF YOU EVERY NIGHT
SHARING EVERYTHING POSSIBLE
EVEN CHANGING DARKNESS TO LIGHT
YOU NEVER CEASE TO AMAZE ME
IT'S THE WAY YOU CONTROL YOUR TOUCH
AN INSPIRATION SO DEEP
THAT'S MAKE ME WANT YOU SO MUCH
YOU KNOW JUST WHAT TO DO
TO BRING ME AROUND
YOU POLISH MY HEART
AND EVEN MY CROWN
AT THIS VERY MOMENT
I SHARE WHAT IS TRUE
I LOVE YOU MY DEAR
FOR YOU
BEING YOU

28)
MY QUEEN TO BE

I CAN TASTE THE MOMENT I MET YOU
VISIONS OF A CANDLE LIGHT BATH
THE MOON AWAITS WITH ESSENCE
THE ROSES LEAD OUR PATH
THE ATMOSPHERE GIVES OFF A SCENT
FROM THE PASSION THAT STARTS TO BOIL
OUR MINDS ARE RELAXED
AS WE GROOM OUR BODIES WITH OIL
ENERGY IS IN EVERY STROKE
I'M PRIVILEGED TO ONLY PLEASE
THE BEAUTY OF YOUR QUALITY
FOR THE LOVE THAT IT ALSO NEEDS
YOU'RE EVERYTHING I'VE DREAMED OF
MY LOVE IS ONLY FOR YOU
I SHOW THE STRONGEST APPRECIATION
THAT YOU ARE SPECIAL, MY BOO
SO LET THE SPIRIT OF LOVE RAIN ON US
LIKE A LAYER OF MORNING DUE
REMEMBERED DEEPLY IN YOUR HEART
THAT MY LOVE IS FOR YOU
ALWAYS TRUE

29)
ONLY WITH YOU

LIGHTLY AS WE GO
GENTLY STROKES
SO TENDER AND SLOW
CARRESSING YOUR BODY
WHISPERING IN YOUR EAR
THE WORDS OF LOVE
AND NOTHING TO FEAR
LOCKED TOGETHER IN EACH OTHERS ARMS
THE SOFTNESS OF YOUR KISS
BRINGS ME ONLY TO REALIZE
THAT IT'S YOU THAT I MISS
TIMES ARE SO BEAUTIFUL
WHEN I'M WITH YOU
MY HEART BEATS WITH A PASSION
FOR WHEN MAKING LOVE IS DUE
LOOKING IN YOUR EYES
YOUR INNOCENCE I FEEL
THE RARENESS OF YOUR QUALITY
SO WARM SO REAL
TONIGHT I WILL DREAM
OF BEING IN THAT SPECIAL PLACE
WHERE I WAS LAST NIGHT
WHEN I SEEN YOUR FACE

30)
THE REASONS WHY

THE REASONS WHY
YOU'RE SO SPECIAL
WHAT I WILL GIVE NOW
TO TOUCH MY BETTER HALF
JUST TO HEAR YOUR SWEET VOICE
OR THE SOUND OF YOUR LAUGH
UNDER SERIOUS DEVASTATION
AND THE FEELLING OF BEING TEASED
MY HEART IS IN A DEEP NEED
OF THE POWER OF BEING PLEASED
YOU'VE BROUGHT MEANING INTO MY LIFE
BY THE WAY YOU SHOW CONCERN
YOU ALWAYS SEEM TO AMAZE ME
HOW MUCH MORE CAN I LEARN?
I'M DEDICATED AND DEVOTED
TO YOUR MENTAL AND PHYSICAL ATTRATION
YOU'RE THE CURE FOR MY HEART
MY EVERY SATISFACTION
I SAY IT WITH ALL HONESTY
THAT YOUR QUALITY IS VERY RARE
IT'S THE WARMTH IN YOUR HEART
THE LOVE THAT WE SHARE
GIFTED WITH SELF RESPECT
FOR YOUR BEAUTY SO VERY NICE
I HAVE TO SAY I LOVE YOU
CAUSE YOU'RE MY ONE AND ONLY SPICE

31)
BELIEVE ME LOVE

WE'VE REACHED THE HIGHEST LEVEL
WHERE OUR LOVE IS AT ITS BEST
WE'VE BEEN THROUGH THE CHANGES
AND NOW WE HAVE BEEN BLESSED
LEARNING AND UNDERSTANDING
ALL THE VALUES OF WHAT WE FEEL
THE SECURITY OF LOVE IN OUR HEARTS
IS THE ANSWER TO WHAT IS REAL
TO HAVE FAITH AND HONESTY
ARE VALUABLE KEYS
FOR IT IS THE GREATEST POWER
THAT EVERY RELATIONSHIP NEEDS
WHAT WE HAVE TOGETHER
PROTECTS THE THINGS THAT ARE RIGHT
IT'S THE GIFT OF GLORY
THAT PROVIDED US WITH LIFE
THERE IS SOMETHING VERY UNIQUE
ABOUT OUR LOVE
IT'S NOURISHED WITH A STRENGTH
THAT COMES FROM ABOVE
TO THINK ABOUT TOMORROW
IS TO HOPE AND PRAY
CAUSE WE CAN ONLY LIVE
DAY BY DAY

32)
LONELINESS

LONELINESS IS A DEEP DARKNESS
WHEN EVERYTHING SEEMS UNFAIR
IT'S A PIERCING SOUND OF A CRY
WHEN NO-ONE ELSE SEEMS TO CARE
ONLY ONE TEAR FOR A COMPANION
WHICH WILL SOON COME TO EVAPORATE
AND THE EMOTIONS WITHIN MY HEART
ARE SEARCHING TO COMMUNICATE
SADENESS HAS OVERCOME ME
LIKE A SPIRIT WITHOUT A SOUL
MY MIND IS IN A TRANCE
THIS FEELING IS GETTING OLD
FROM THE WEDGES OF SEPERATION
OUT OF DISTANCE OF TENDERNESS AND TOUCH
JUST THE FEEL THAT YOU'RE LISTENING
IS INSPIRING AND MEANS SO MUCH
FROM THE DEEPEST DEPTH OF SOLUTUDE
LONELLINESS I HOPE TO END
LEAVING MY AFFECTION ONLY WONDERING
IF I CAN EVER TRUST AGAIN
LONELINESS HAS ITS PENALITIES
IT TAKES WITHOUT CONCERN
AND THE JUDGEMENTS THAT WE MAKE
ARE THE MISTAKES THAT WE LEARN

33)
THE CURRENT

AS I CLOSE MY EYES
I THINK OF THINGS TO FEEL
THE SOFTNESS OF YOUR SKIN
SO WARM SO REAL
I WANT TO TOUCH YOU DESPERATELY
RUN MY FINGERS THROUGH YOUR HAIR
WHISPERING THOSE PRECIOUS WORDS
OF TENDER LOVING CARE
MAKING LOVE IS ON MY MIND
TO RELEASE THAT NATURAL FLOW
TO FERTILIZE THE BEAUTY
WITH THE SPICES FOR OUR LOVE TO GROW
NOTHING WILL BREAK MY VOW
THE DEDICATION OF LOVE FOR YOU
WILL STAND FIRM WITH ALL LOYALTY
AND A FAITH THAT IS ALSO TRUE
YOUR BEAUTY IS OF GREAT VALUE
INSIDE AND OUT I BELIEVE
THAT YOU ARE THE GOLDEN ANGEL
WHO CAME TO SET ME FREE
EVERYDAY AND EVERY NIGHT
YOU'RE ALWAYS ON MY MIND
SO SWEET, SO PRECIOUS
SO GENTLE, SO DEVINE

34)
THE HEAT

IT'S YOUR VOICE I HEAR SO SOFTLY
YOUR HEART I FEEL WITH MINE
I WISH I COULD TURN UP THE VOLUME
BEFORE IT MELTS IN MY MIND
OUR LOVE IS GROWING WITH A PASSION
WHICH I HOPE TO NEVER REGRET
EVEN AT THIS VERY MOMENT
YOU MAKE ME HOT AND SILKY WET
I CAN TASTE YOUR LOVE SO SWEETLY
WHAT I VALUE IN MY HEART IS TRUE
I SPENT A LOT OF TIME TOSSING AND TURNING
BECAUSE MY APPETITE IS ONLY FOR YOU
MAKING LOVE TO YOU IS WHAT I FEEL
BOLDLY AND SHOWING NO SHAME
AS THE SWEAT BREAKS DOWN MY BACK
FROM THE SOUND OF YOU CALLING MY NAME
STROKING IN THE MOMENT OF GENTLENESS
WHISPERING IN EACH OTHERS EAR
IT'S YOUR VOICE I HEAR SO SOFTLY
AND YOUR FACE I SEE SO CLEAR

35)
SHE IS SWEET AND SILENT

I CAN FEEL THE HEAT
OF A DEEP BURNING FIRE
A WARM SECURITY
FOR THE QUALITY OF DESIRE
GIFTED WITH A TALENT
SPIRITUALLY IN TOUCH
WITH HIGHER ABILITIES
THAT OFFER SO MUCH
LOYAL AND FAITHFUL
WITH DEEP SENSITIVE EYES
HOLDING THE SHADOWS OF HER PAST
A HISTORY THAT CRIES
DEDICATED AND DEVOTED
TO LOVE, CARE, AND CONCERN
SHE GIVES FULL NOURISHMENT
FOR INSPIRATION TO LEARN
SHE'S THE QUEEN OF CREATION
WHO CARESSES ALL NEEDS
HER RESPECT FOR NATURE
HOLDS THE VALUES OF DEEDS
SHE'S THE BLESSING OF LIFE
A FACE IN A CLOUD
A VOICE TO BE HEARD
WHERE SILENCE SEEMS SO LOUD

36)
IN THE MIDDLE

I JUST WANT TO MAKE YOU FEEL
LIKE TIME HAS JUST BEGUN
TO MAKE YOU ONLY FEEL LIKE
YOU'RE EVERYTHING UNDER THE SUN
YOU'RE CONSTANTLY ON MY MIND
MY HEART IS READY TO EXPLORE
THE CHAMBERS OF YOUR LOVE
YOU'RE PASSION AND EVEN MORE
I WANT TO SHOW YOU I CARE
I TRULY BELIEVE THAT I'M READY
TO HOLD YOU CLOSE, HOLD YOU TIGHT
SO CLOSE TO ME, HOLD YOU STEADY
WITH A DEEP INTENSE DESIRE
ONLY YOU I AIM TO PLEASE
WITH THE DILEVERANCE OF TRUE PASSION
LASTING FOREVER AND NEVER TO CEASE
I WANT TO FEEL DEEP INSIDE OF YOU
SO MUCH PRESSURE TO UNWIND
FOR SUCH A BEAUTIFUL LOVE
IS SO VERY HARD TO FIND

37)
SUMMER TIME

A NICE BEAUTIFUL DAY
NATURES CREATED SCENE
THE TREES ARE FULL
THE GRASS IS GREEN
HAPPINESS IS IN THE AIR
THE SUN IS SHINNING
CHILDREN ARE PLAYING
LAUGHING AND UNWINDING
A NICE WARM BREEZE
FEELING GOOD TO THE SKIN
PEOPLE GATHERING TOGETHER
SHARING GOOD TIMES AGAIN
PICNICS, BAR-B-QUE'S
MUSIC AND SMILES
CARNIVALS AND FESTIVALS
TRAVLING FOR MILES
IT'S THE TIME OF THE YEAR
FOR HAVING SO MUCH FUN
PARTYING BY THE LAKES
AND ENJOYING THE SUN

38)
HAPPY BIRTHDAY

THERE ARE SO MANY BEAUTIFUL THINGS
THAT COME WITH THE SEASONS
SO MANY GREATFUL THINGS
WITH BLESSINGS AND REASONS
THIS IS A SPECIAL DAY
TO PUT A SMILE ON YOUR FACE
CAUSE I WILL GIVE ANYTHING
TO BE IN YOUR PLACE
AS BROTHER AND SISTER
FAMILY AND FRIEND
WE SHARE A LOVE THAT WILL
NEVER PART AND NEVER END
SO MAKE THIS DAY A SPECIAL DAY
THAT YOU'VE BEEN BLESSED TO LIVE
I'M SENDING YOU MY HEART
AND ALL I CAN GIVE
JUST REMEMBER THAT TRUE LOVE
IN THE MOST PRECIOUS WAY
SAYS THANK YOU FOR YOUR LOVE
AND HAPPY BIRTHDAY

39)
HAPPY HOLIDAYS

WE LIVE BY THE SEASONS
IN GROWTH WE CHANGE
TO ACCEPT THE PURITIES OF BLESSINGS
THAT ARE WELL ARRANGED
AS WE SHARE LAUGHS AND SMILES
SENDING OUT SPECIAL GIFTS
THAT TRAVEL FOR MILES
MAKING OUR DEDICATIONS
TO THOSE WE SO LOVE AND MISS
GIVING INTO THE GRACE
OF A HUG OR A KISS
TO SHARE THIS MOMENT WITH YOU
IS A VISION SO CLEAR
THE FEELING OF TRUE WARMTH
OF A HEART SO NEAR
THE NEW YEAR HAS COME
LOVE AND HAPPINESS WE SHARE
SPECIAL THOUGHTS OF CONCERN
OF TENDER LOVING CARE
TO YOU I SEND MY BLESSINGS
I VALUE IN A SPECIAL WAY
HOPING THAT EVERYTHING IS GOING WELL
HAPPY HOLIDAY

40)
APPRECIATION FOR MOTHERS

TO HONOR YOU DEARELY
FOR SHARING WITH US YOU'RE HEART
THE BEAUTY OF YOUR QUALITY
WILL NEVER FALL APART
HOW GREATFUL IS YOUR RESPECT
SENSITIVE VALUES TO ADORE
YOU'RE STRENGTH OFFERS CONCERN
WITH A FLAVOR WITH LOVE AND MORE
ONE TIME FOR YOUR INSPIRATION
TWO TIMES FOR YOUR PRAISE
YOU'RE EVERYTHING WITHIN MY HEART
A WITNESS FOR ALL OF MY DAYS
CREATION HAS BROUGHT ME HAPPINESS
WITH ALL THE LOVE TO RECEIVE
THE PURENESS OF YOUR SECURITY
I'LL ALWAYS BELIEVE
I ONLY WANT TO THANK GOD
FOR BRINGING AN ANGEL DOWN
TO SHINE THE LIGHT ON THE BEAUTY
OF THE MOTHERS WHO HOLD THEIR CROWN

41)
FRIENDSHIP

FRIENDSHIP IS A KEY VALUE
WHEN EVERYTHING SEEMS UNFAIR
IT'S THE BRIDGE OF COMMUNICATION
A SPECIAL WAY TO CARE
FRIENDSHIP IS THE BUILDING OF TRUST
THE TRUTH NEEDS NO DEFENDING
THE LOYALTY OF ITS NATURE
IS LIMITLESS AND NEVER ENDING
FRIENDSHIP OFFERS UNDERSTANDING
WITH A DEEP MEANS OF CONCERN
IT HOLDS STRENGTH AND SECURITY
NEVER HESITATES TO LEARN
FRIENDSHIP IS SOMETHING RARE
SOMEONE WHO'S ALWAYS THERE
IT'S THE JOY AND HAPPINESS GIVEN
AND MANY OTHER THINGS TO SHARE
FRIENDSHIP IS A TRUE BLESSING
OF A GIFT SO REAL
I SAY IT WITH ALL HONESTY
THAT IN YOU THESE THINGS I FEEL

42)
LIES

THERE'S A DEEP CONTROVERSY
BEHIND THE POWER OF LIES
THAT CAN BREAK A HEART DOWN
CAUSE THE INNOCENT TO CRY
LIES ARE THE LINKS
BEHIND THE THINGS THAT ARE RIGHT
BUT THERE ALWAYS COMES A TIME
FOR THE TRUTH TO SHED LIGHT
LIES CAN CAUSE BETRAYAL
LEAVE A LIFE INCOMPLETE
THE PRETENDING OF BEING REAL
CAN CAUSE THE MIND TO LOOSE SLEEP
LIES OFFERS NO VALLUES
THEY ADD AND MULITPLY
SOME ARE BEING TOLD
WITHOUT THE REASONS OF KNOWING WHY
LIES COMES IN ALL FORMS
COLORS AND RACES
SOMETIMES IT HAS A WAY
OF EXPRESSIONS ON FACES
TO BE LIVING A LIE
IS TO BE A FACE UNKNOWN
STANDING OUT IN THE CROWD
BY YOURSELF AND ALL ALONE

43)
MONEY

THE CAPITOL OF EVIL
RULER OF FINANCIAL GAIN
IN GOD WE TRUST
WHO WROTE THAT? INSANE
THE POWER OF MONEY
WILL MAKE ONE CROSS HIS OWN
DISTORT A FAMILY
RECK A HOUSE AND A HOME
MONEY HAS THE POWER
TO BRING STRONG MATERIAL WEALTH
CAUSING DISTRUCTION, SUICIDE
AND POOR HEALTH
MONEY CAN MAKE YOU STRONG
TURN AROUND AND MAKE YOU WEAK
FROM THE SINFUL DESIRES
THAT THE UNCONSCIOUS SEEK
THE REALITY OF HAVING MONEY
IS TO TRULY UNDERSTAND
THAT IT CAN NEVER SAVE YOU
AND IT DOESN'T MAKE A MAN

44)
HUMBLENESS AND RECOVERY

A TRANSFORMATION THAT TAKES PLACE
BY A PEACEFULL SUBMISSION
TO THE TERMS OF ACCEPTANCE
AN HONEST CONFESSION
IT DISCOVERS THE TRUE IDENTITY
OF THE REAL PERSON DEEP INSIDE
BRINGING OUT INTO THE OPEN
THE THINGS YOU'RE TRYING TO HIDE
IT FINDS THE COURAGE TO FORGIVE
WHATEVER DAMAGES THAT WERE DONE
THE HIGHER-SELF AND THE LOWER-SELF
COME TOGETHER AS ONE
THEN COMES THE PROCESS OF ALLIGNMENT
A SPIRITUAL WALK
THAT FOLLOWS IN ACCORDANCE
WITH THE WAY YOU TALK
PURPOSE COMES TO LIFE
FOR WHAT YOU'VE BEEN CREATED FOR
AND IGNITES A STRONG WILL
TO WANT TO LOVE YOURSELF MORE
WHAT USE TO KEEP YOU DOWN
YOU NOW STAND ABOVE
A MANIFESTED THOUGHT
A DEFINITION OF LOVE

45)
IT'S OVER

YOU'VE TRIED TO RUIN MY LIFE
NO LONGER CAN I STAY
I CAN'T TAKE THE TEMPTATION
OF THE DIRTY GAMES YOU PLAY
YOU SAY YOU HAVE RESPECT
BUT I CAN'T TELL
SO I HAVE TO GO MY WAY
ALTHOUGH I DO WISH YOU WELL
TO BAD IT COULDN'T HAVE BEEN BETTER
HERE'S YOUR RECIEPT
FOR MAKING MY LIFE MISERABLE
AND SO DAM INCOMPLETE
I NEVER WOULD HAVE WROTE THIS
BUT I'M REALLY KIND OF SHOOK
YOU LIED FROM THE BEGINNING
TAKE MY NAME OUT OF YOUR BOOK
THINGS COULD HAVE BEEN SWEETER
BUT YOU CHOSE TO BE A WITCH
YOU DON'T KNOW WHAT YOU'RE MISSING
CAUSE I'VE FINALLY MADE IT RICH
IT IS IN MY HEART TO BELIEVE
THERE'S ALWAYS A BETTER WAY
IT'S OVER!!!!
AND THERE'S NOTHING YOU CAN SAY

46)
FACING REALITY

I SPENT A LOT TIME IN THOUGHT
WONDERING AND CHASING DREAMS
TO REALIZE MY PURPOSE
AND DEFINITION OF WHAT IT MEANS
OFTEN TIED UP IN GAMES
SOME PLAY AND SOME RESPECTED
BEING CAUGHT UP IN THIS SYSTEM
WAS THE LAST THING I EXPECTED
ROLLING HIGH WITH SELFISH DESIRES
TRAPPED IN A WORLD OF FANTASY
IT WAS THE MENTAL IMPACT
OF WHAT MY LIFE MEANT TO ME
BUT IT CAME TO A TIME
TO PULL OUT OF THE RACE
RESTORING A NEW LIFE
AND GIVING THE GAME ITS SPACE
THERE ARE OTHER THINGS POSITIVE
LIFE OFFERS WITH A GUARANTEE
LIKE BEING AT HOME
TAKING CARE OF FAMILY
WITH ANOTHER CHANCE AT LIFE
HAVING A WHOLE NEW PLAN
IS BEING HONEST WITH YOU
AND MORE FIRM I WILL STAND

47)
IT'S TOO LATE

THE HAMMER IS ALREADY COCKED
I SEE BLURY VISIONS OF RED
IT WAS THE FRUSTRATION IN MY HEART
THE MISSION OF BLOOD SHED
LIFE WAS ALWAYS DARK
I PROWLED THROUGH THE NIGHT
SLEPT DURING THE DAY
UNTIL THE TIME WAS RIGHT
BUT THEN SOMETHING HAPPENED
THAT PUT MY LIFE IN A JAM
I KNEW IF IT HIT THE SURFACE
MY WHOLE LIFE WOULD BE SLAMMED
WITHOUT A EDUCATION
I'VE SPENT MY LIFE ON THE BLOCKS
NOW I'M DUCKING AND DODGING
HIDING BEHIND CORNERS AND ROCKS
NEVER COULD BE PRESENT
I HAD TO WHISPER OR WHISTLE
EVERYWHERE I WENT
MY ONLY FRIEND WAS MY PISTOLE
STARTED OFF AS A HUSTLER
ADVANCED INTO STEALING
NOW I'M A VETREAN
A HARD CORE VILLAN
IT'S A SAD THING TO SAY
FOR MY LIFE IS ON THE RUN
CAUSE IF THEY CATCH ME NOW
I'LL NEVER SEE THE SUN

48)
THE CAGE

LOOKING THROUGH THE BARS
I ACKNOWLEDGED THE GLORY OF RAIN
AS I FIGHT THE AGONY
AND THE MENTAL COMPACITY OF PAIN
MY DAYS ARE GROWING SHORTER
SOON I WILL BE FREE
EFFECTIVE AND STRONG
WITH A DIFFERENT MENTALITY
SAFE AND SECURED
FROM THE SPIRIT ABOVE
MY HEART HAS THE GIFT
OF THE POWER OF MUCH LOVE
MY MIND IS GROWING STRONG
WITH A EDUCATIONAL ABILITY
IT HELPS ME TO BE CONTENT
DEAL WITH LIFES REALITY
IT WILL SURE BE NICE TO TOUCH
MY EMOTIONAL DESISRES
TO BE HOME WITH MY FAMILY
IS WHAT MY HEART INSPIRSES
BRAND NEW AND FRESH
WITH MORE THAN ENOUGH TO GAIN
IF I EVER END UP BACK HERE AGAIN
IT'S BECAUSE I'M INSANE

49)
PATIENCE

I'VE WAITED FOR SO VERY LONG
FOR THIS MOMENT TO COME TRUE
THERE NEVER WAS A DAY THAT WENT BY
THAT I DIDN'T THINK OF YOU
SO MANY NIGHTS I LAY AWAKE
YOUR VOICE DANCING IN MY MIND
SEEING PICTURES OF YOUR FACE
I NOW SEEK TO FIND
THERE WERE TIMES WHERE I FELF LOST
AND DIDN'T KNOW WHAT TO DO
I CRIED DESPERATLY OUT LOUD
FOR FAITH TO SEE ME THROUGH
I KNEW DEEP IN MY HEART
THAT IF THIS IS MEANT TO BE
YOU WOULD COME INTO MY LIFE
AND SET MY PAIN FREE
TOGETHER WE WILL BE FOREVER
FOR THIS IS NOT A DREAM
CAUSE LOVE RISES TO THE TOP
LIKE THE TEXTURE OF CREAM

50)
STRUGGLES

AT TIMES WE STRUGGLE
CAUSE SOMETIMES WERE IN DOUBT
IN SOME SITUATIONS
IT'S TO DEVELOPE CLOUT
SETTING GOALS AND MAKING ACHIEVEMENTS
MATERIAL WEALTH OR FINANCIAL GAIN
THE RISK AND CHALLENGES MAY CAUSE
A GREAT INDURANCE OF PAIN
IT BUILDS UP A CHARACTER OF INTERGRITY
TO BE CREATIVE, DESIGN, AND PLAN
IT'S THE BALANCE OF LIFE
FOR EVERY WOMAN AND MAN
SOMETIMES WE HAVE THE TENDENCIES
TO HARBOR AND NOT LET GO
FINDING OURSELVES FIGHTING
WITH THE THINGS BEYOND OUR CONTROL
IN STRUGGLING WE UNDERSTAND
MANY VALUES ARE EARNED
FROM TRIALS AND TRIBULATIONS
MANY LESSONS ARE LEARNED
IT'S KNOWING HOW TO BALANCE
YOUR RIGHT, YOUR WRONG
AND AT YOUR WEAKEST POINT
THAT'S WHEN YOU BECOME STRONG

51)
BEING THOUGHT OF

AT TIMES IT FEELS GOOD TO BE NEEDED
SOMETIMES BEING THOUGHT OF
IT'S NOTHING MORE BEAUTIFUL TO EMBRACE
THAN THE POWER OF LOVE
IT'S A GOD GIVEN BLESSING
TO BE ABLE TO GIVE AND ACHIEVE
OFFERING SO MUCH MORE
THAN WE EXPECT TO RECEIVE
SOMETIMES WE NEED TO KNOW
THAT SOMEONE TRULY CARES
NOT BECAUSE OF POPULARITY
OR HIGH CLASS AFFAIRS
IT DOESN'T HAVE TO BE VERY MUCH
A CARD, A LETTER, A SIMPLE HELLO
CAN GIVE SOMEONE ELSE
THE MOST OUTSTANDING GLOW
THERE'S NOTHING MORE BEAUTIFUL
THAN BEING THOUGHT OF
AND BEING ABLE TO EMBRACE
THE POWER OF LOVE

52)
HERE MY PRAYER

O'LORD YOU ARE MY FOUNDATION
MY HEART HAS FULLY ADDRESSED
RELEASE ME FROM THE HANDS OF THOSE
WHO CONTINUE TO KEEP ME PRESSED
WITH MY BACK TO THE WORLD
MY FACE I LOOK UP TO YOU
I HAVE NO STRENGTH OF MY OWN
BUT YOU ARE CAPABLE AND TRUE
FOR SO MANY YEARS I'VE SEARCHED
ALL THE WHILE YOU WERE THERE
FORGIVE ME OF MY SINS
FOR TREATING YOU SO UNFAIR
IN TIMES OF MY DISTRESS
YOU'VE ALWAYS HAD A HAND ON ME
SO LET YOUR FAVOR CONTINUE TO INCREASE
IF IT IS THY WILL TO BE
I SECURE MYSELF WITHIN THE COMFORT
OF THY TRUTH AND POWERFUL MIGHT
THAT WHATEVER I MAY HAVE TO FACE
WILL ONLY BE JUDGED BY RIGHT
O'LORD YOU ARE MY FOUNDATION
HEAR MY PRAYER CALLING OUT TO THEE
CAUSE YOU ARE MY SALAVATION
THE ONLY LIGHT I SEE

53)
PROVIDE FOR ME

PROVIDE FOR ME LORD
THE WORDS TO SPEAK WHAT IS WISE
ALLOW ME TO SEE
ONLY THROUGH YOUR EYES
PROVIDE FOR ME LORD
THE KNOWLEDGE TO UNDERSTAND
YOUR HOLY MESSAGE
THE LAW OF YOUR COMMAND
PROVIDE FOR ME LORD
AN ARMOR OF PROTECTION
YOUR EVERLASTING LIGHT
FOR THE PURPOSE OF DIRECTION
PROVIDE FOR ME LORD
THE GIFT TO DISCERN
THE RIGHT FROM THE WRONG
THE WILL TO LEARN
PROVIDE FOR ME LORD
MY DESIRE MY EVERY NEED
ALL THE SPIRITUAL FOOD
TO FERTILIZE YOUR SEED
PROVIDE FOR ME LORD
I CAN NOT DO IT ALONE
YOU ARE MY FOUNDATION
MY ROCK, MY STONE

54)
YOUR EXSISTENCE

SUNSHINE IS THE LIGHT OF YOUR EYES
THAT GLOWS UPON MY FACE
YOUR TEARS ARE THE RIVERS THAT FLOW
FROM PLACE TO PLACE
THE THUNDER IS YOUR VOICE
THAT TRIMBLES THE MOUNTAINS AND THE TREES
WITH YOUR BREATH YOU CREATE THE WINDS
AND A SILENT BREEZE
WITH ONLY ONE SPOKEN WORD
A VARIETY OF LIFE BECAME
THE POWER OF YOUR THOUGHT
GAVE EVERYTHING A NAME
WITH THE WAVE OF THY HAND
YOU GAVE THE ELEMENTS A FORM
WHEN SOME COME IN SILENCE
OTHERS COME IN A STORM
YOUR THOUGHTS REVEAL THE TRUTH
FROM THE BEGINNING TO THE END
EVERYTHIG THAT WAS, IS, AND NOW
ONLY FEW CAN COMPREHEND

55)
PRAYER

AS THIS DAY BEGINS TO UNFOLD
LEAD ME BY YOUR LIGHT
IN YOUR HAND MY LIFE YOU HOLD
SO HELP ME TO DO WHAT IS RIGHT
COVER ME WITH YOUR BLANKET
OF LOVE AND PROTECTION
PROVIDE ME WITH THE UNDERSTANDING
OF WISDOM AND DIRECTION
LET IT BE YOUR SIGNATURE
THAT AUTHORIZES MY PATH
THOSE WHO PLAN EVIL AGAINST ME
WILL FILL THE POWER OF THY WRATH
ALLOW ME TO BE USED TODAY
AS A FOUNTAIN OF LIFE
ENGRAVE IN ME A MESSAGE
THAT IS AS SHARP AS A KNIFE
MY LOVE FOR YOU LORD
REACHES OUT TO TOUCH OTHERS
SO SHINE THROUGH ME LORD
ON THE FACES OF MY SISTERS AND BROTHERS
IN EVERYTHING I DO
EVERY SECOND, EVERY MINUTE AND EVERY HOUR
I THANK YOU FOR YOUR LOVE
YOUR MERCY, YOUR GRACE AND POWER

56)
DEAR LORD

BEFORE I RISE OUT OF BED
THERE'S SO MUCH I THANK YOU FOR
AS I EMBRACE YOU IN MY HEART
MY LOVE CONTINUES TO POUR
LET THE SPIRIT OF YOUR HOLINESS
SHINE GREATLY UPON MY FACE
IF THERE'S ANYTHING UNHEALTHY WITHIN
LET YOUR HEALING TAKE PLACE
FORGIVE ME OF ALL MY SINS
THE GRIND AND THE UGLY CRUD
PURIFY YOUR HOLY TEMPLE
WITH THE CLEANSING OF THY BLOOD
IN SILENCE OH LORD I PRAY
BEFORE MY FEET TOUCH THE GROUND
SHIELD ME WITH THE ARMOR OF PROTECTION
FROM THE EVIL THAT LEARKS AROUND
THANK YOU FOR BREATHING ON ME
ANOTHER BEAUTIFUL DAY
I LIVE BECAUSE OF YOUR WILL
IN YOUR NAME LORD I PRAY

57)
LET GO AND LET GOD

LET GO AND LET GOD
IS THE RIGHTEOUS WAY TO GO
STOP FIGHTING WITH ISSUES
THAT ARE OUT OF YOUR CONTROL
LET GO AND LET GOD
BE THE HEAD OF YOUR LIFE
TO HELP YOU FIGHT THE BATTLES
OF TRIBULATION AND STRIFE
LET GO AND LET GOD
IS TO TAKE A RIGHTEOUS STAND
TO UNDERSTAND THE LAW
AND THE STRUCTURE OF HIS PLAN
LET GO AND LET GOD
IS TO SURRENDER AND RELEASE
ALL SELF CONTROL
FOR THE COMFORT OF PEACE
LET GO AND LET GOD
TOTALLY LEAD THE WAY
AND GIVE THANKS FOR THE CHANCE
TO SEE ANOTHER DAY

58)
WORRING AND MISERY

WORRING AND MISERY
IS A POWERFUL COMBINATION
OF SO MUCH TENSION
SO MUCH FRUSTRATION
WORRING CAN SOMETIMES
BRING ON THE MOST DEVASTATING PAIN
MISERY WITHIN ITSELF
CAN DRIVE A PERSON INSANE
WORRING CAN SOMETIMES
CAUSE A LACK TO COMMUNICATE
FROM A BOILING POINT OF ANGER
AND A BURNING PASSION OF HATE
WORRING CAN SOMETIMES
CAUSE YOU TO BE BLIND
MISERY WILL NOT LET YOU
SEEK NOR FIND
WORRING AND MISERY AT TIMES
CAN BE FOR THE SAKE OF LOVE
BUT WHO CAN HANDLE THEM BOTH
BETTER THAN THE ONE ABOVE

59)
THE ATTACK

AS I GROW CLOSER TO GOD
A DEGREE OF SUFFERING IS TAKING PLACE
BECAUSE I CHOOSE TO LIVE RIGHT
BY THE WILL OF HIS GRACE
I REALIZE AT THIS POINT
THAT A CONTRACT IS OUT FOR MY LIFE
FROM THE WICKED CONFUSION
OF DESTRUCTION AND STRIFE
I HAVE TO KEEP ON FIGHTING
I HAVE A MESSAGE TO SPREAD
THE BODY IS NO GOOD
WITHOUT THE HEAD
FROM MY FAMILY TO MY POSSESSIONS
EVEN MY SOUL
THERE'S NO COMPROMISING
WITH MY ULTIMATE GOAL
I SEEK THE WILL OF GOD
BY WHATEVER MEANS IT MAY COST
AND ALL THAT IS GONE
DOESN'T MEAN THAT IT'S LOST

60)
LORD

HAS ANYONE EVER TOLD YOU
TO HAVE A NICE DAY
WELL AT THIS VERY MOMENT
THAT'S WHAT I PRAY
YOU'RE ALWAYS SO BUSY
HANDLING SO MANY AFFAIRS
CIRCUMSTANCES AND SITUATIONS
ANSWERING PRAYERS
WE ALWAYS SEEM TO COME TO YOU
WHEN TIMES GET TOUGH
I REALLY FEEL TRULY
WE DON'T PRAISE YOU ENOUGH
I CAN'T IMAGINE THE PETITIONS
THE PRAYERS BUILDING UP
OF ALL WHO WANT BLESSINGS
TO OVERFLOW THEIR CUP
TODAY OH LORD I WILL
QUALITY TIME I FIND
TO COME TOGETHER WITH YOU
IN SPIRIT, SOUL, AND MIND
THANKING YOU FOR THE BLESSINGS
AND ALL THE LOVE YOU SERVE
GIVING YOU MY HONOR
AND ALL THE LOVE YOU DESERVE

61)
WHO IS IN THE MIRROR

WHEN YOU LOOK IN THE MIRROR
DO YOU REALLY KNOW WHO YOU ARE?
OR ARE YOU JUST AN EXAMPLE
OF ANOTHER FALLING STAR
WHEN YOU LOOK IN THE MIRROR
BEHIND THE CURTAINS OF YOUR EYES
DO YOU SEE SOMETHING UGLY?
OR SOMETHING BEAUTIFUL AND WISE
WHEN YOU LOOK IN THE MIRROR
DOES YOUR FACE MATCH YOUR NAME?
OR IS IT JUST ANOTHER IMAGE
OF A MUNIPULATIVE GAME
WHEN YOU LOOK IN THE MIRROR
DO YOU SEE SOMETHING GOOD
OR ARE YOU STEADY TELLING YOURSELF
IF I COULD I WOULD
WHEN YOU LOOK IN THE MIRROR
CAN YOU TELL BETWEEN THE TWO
IF YOU'RE LIVING FOR SOMEONE ELSE
OR LIVING FOR YOU

62)
THE MASTER OF DESIGN

AT FIRST THERE WAS DARKNESS
THEN THERE WAS LIGHT
ONE WAS CALLED DAY
THE OTHER WAS CALLED NIGHT
THE MOST BEAUTIFUL THING
SUDDENLY CAME TO BIRTH
A MANIFESTED THOUGHT
CREATED A WORLD CALLED EARTH
THEN THERE WAS A MOMENT
A STYLE OF ROTATION
TIME BECAME THE EVIDENCE
FOR THE PURPOSE OF CREATION
WITH THE TOUCH OF PERFECTION
TO ADD TO THE PLAN
FROM THE DUST OF THE GROUND
BECAME A FORM OF MAN
FROM THE BREATH OF THE SPIRIT
THIS MAN WAS GIVEN LIFE
AND FROM THE RIB OF HIS BODY
HE WAS BLESSED WITH A WIFE

63)
GRATITUDE

*GIVING ALL PRAISE, GLORY AND HONOR TO GOD AND
TO THE LORD JESUS CHRIST I THANK YOU FOR THE
BREATH OF LIFE FOR KEEPING YOUR HANDS ON ME
THROUGH A JOURNEY OF EXPERIENCES FOR THE HEALTH
THAT YOU KEEP ME IN BEING ABLE TO WALK TALK SEE
AND HEAR. I THANK YOU FOR THE KNOWLEDGE, AND
WISDOM, MY WIFE, MY CHILDREN, MY MOTHER AND
FATHER, AND MY BROTHER AND SISTERS, GRANDPARENTS
AND FOR FATHERS, FOR THE PEOPLE OF GOD, AND
ALSO FOR MY ENEMIES, THE DRUGS AND ALCOHOL,
PRISON, FOOD, WATER AND FOR THE TRIALS AND
TRIBULATIONS, PROTECTION, LOVE, CARE, MERCY,
PATIENCE, CHESTISMENTS, UNDERSTANDING AND THE
GIFT OF DICERNMENT. I THANK YOU FOR EMPLOYMENT,
TREATMENT PROGRAMS, LEADERS AND FOLLOWERS. I
THANK YOU FOR SHOES, CLOTHES, TRANSPORTATION,
MY SANITY, THE GIFT TO WRITE, THE LAND, THE WATERS
AND ALL THE BEAUTIFUL CREATURES THAT WALK,
CRAWL, FLY AND SWIM. I THANK YOU FOR HOPE, FAITH,
LOVE, PEACE, AND FOR THE FREEDOM OF CHOICE, FOR
HOMES, HOSPITALS, CHURCHES, AND SCHOOLS. I THANK
YOU FOR THE BIBLE AND FOR HAVING FAVOR IN ME AND
FOR THE GIFT OF ETERNAL LIFE. I THANK YOU FOR THE
THINGS THAT I'M NOT CAPABLE OF ASKING FOR. I THANK
YOU FOR MY SAVIOR,
THE LORD JESUS CHRIST, AMEN*

(64)
SO BEAUTIFUL

DARK AND LOVELY
SO BEAUTIFUL AND DEVINE
WITH A DEEP DESIRE
I WISH THAT YOU WERE MINE
SOFT SILKY HAIR
DEEP ATTRACTIVE EYES
A PERSONALITY SO BEAUTIFUL
WITH NO HIDDEN DISQUISE
THE TEXTURE OF SKIN SO TENDER
SENSITIVE VALUES TO ADORE
YOU'RE EVERYTHING IN A WOMAN
THAT I'VE BEEN LOOKING FOR
YOU SPEAK WITH A SOFT TONGUE
A MISTIFYING HEART OF GOLD
WHAT YOU HAVE IS PRICELESS
COULD NEVER BE BOUGHT OR SOLD
YOU ARE SO BEAUTIFUL
SO SWEET AND SO FINE
I LOVE YOU LADY
CAUSE YOUR RICH LIKE SLOW WINE

65)
TRUST ME

TRUST IS A VALUE
THAT IS WARM WITH INSPIRATION
AND HOLDS A DEEP CLOSENESS
OF A BRIDGE OF COMMUNICATION
TRUST IS A VALUE
OF FAITH AND SECURITY
IT BRINGS OUT THE BEST
OF THE GREATEST NOBILITY
TRUST IS A VALUE
OF A CARESSING EMBRACE
IT'S ALWAYS THERE TO MEET YOU
ANYTIME OR ANY PLACE
TRUST IS A VALUE
THAT TREATS EVERYTHING FAIR
IT SHOWS DEEP AFFECTION
WITH TENDER LOVING CARE
TRUST IS A VALUE
A VERY VALUABLE KEY
AND ALL OF THESE THINGS
YOU CAN TRULY FIND IN ME

66)
I'M SO GLAD YOUR MINE

DEDICATED AND MOLDED
SO PRESIOUS AND DEVINE
SO SWEET AND TENDER
SO BEAUTIFUL AND FINE
IF YOU ONLY KNEW
ABOUT THE THINGS YOU DO TO ME
IT TAKES ME TO ANOTHER LEVEL
MAKES ME FEEL FREE
WITH SO MUCH WARMTH
COMPASSION AND DESIRE
YOU NOURISH MY HEART
WITH THE LOVE YOU INSPIRE
I CAN SO APPRECIATE
A LOVE SO TRUE
THERE'S SOMETHING VERY SPECIAL
ABOUT EVERYTHING YOU DO
I FEEL TRULY BLESSED
TO HAVE SOMEONE SO BEAUTIFUL AND DEVINE
AS YOU MY DEAR LADY
I'M SO GLAD YOUR MINE

67)
SAVE YOURSELF

WE WERE ALL MADE WITH PERFECTION
UNTIL SIN BECAME A FLAW
SALVATION CAME TO BE REDEEMED
BY THE OBEDIENCE OF LAW
TO RECEIVE THE ONE AND ONLY
THE MOST ULTIMATE PRICE
YOU MUST CONFESS, REPENT
YOURSELF, SACRAFICE
STAY CLEAR OF YOUR SINFUL NATURE
LISTEN TO THE HOLY VOICE
OF THE ONE WHO GAVE YOU TALENT
A GIFT, THE FREEDOM OF CHOICE
AT TIMES WHERE THERE'S DARKNESS
YOU WILL BE THE LIGHT
ALTHOUGH MANY WILL HATE YOU
FOR STANDING ON WHAT IS RIGHT
DOWN THE HIGHWAY OF LIFE
THERE'S A FORK IN THE PATH
ONE LEADS TO PEACE
THE OTHER TO WRATH
NOW IS THE TIME TO DECIDE
WHICH WAY TO GO
LIKE A THEIF IN THE NIGHT
THE LORD WILL SOON SHOW
AMEN

68)
AN HONEST MAN

I WANT TO BE TRULY
AN HONEST MAN
I WILL BE YOUR SLAVE
OH BABY PLEASE UNDERSTAND
IF THERE'S EVER A MOMENT
WHERE LOVE IS A CRIME
LET IT BE WITH YOU
FOR A LIFE TIME
FOR IF I SHALL DIE
BEFORE THIS SHOULD COME TRUE
IN THE NEXT WORLD I'LL WAIT
TO ONLY BE WITH YOU
I WILL DO WHAT YOU WANT
TO MEET YOUR LOVING DEMAND
AND ALWAYS BE WHERE YOU NEED ME
IN YOUR HEART, AN HONEST MAN

69)
RAIN DROPS OF LOVE

SUDDENLY I WAS AWAKENED
BY THE MOST FAMILIAR SOUND
WHEN I LOOKED OUTSIDE MY WINDOW
THERE WAS MOISTURE ON THE GROUND
WHAT WAS ONCE A BROKEN HEART
AND SO FULL OF PAIN
IS NOW FILLED WITH LOVE
AND DANCING IN THE RAIN
A VISION OF YOU BECAME CLEAR
MY THOUGHTS I BEGAN TO TRACE
OF ALL THE BEAUTIFUL MOMENTS
THE PRETTY SMILE ON YOUR FACE
INSTANTLY I CAME TO REALIZE
THE MUSIC OF THE RAIN WAS NO MORE
THAT'S WHEN THE LOVE IN MY HEART FOR YOU
SUDDENLY STARTED TO POUR
LIKE THE FLOW OF A WATERFALL
HEAVILY TOUCHING THE GROUND
THE RAIN DROPS OF LOVE FOR YOU
MADE SUCH A BEAUTIFUL SOUND

70)
MY MAN

SO HANDSOME AND FINE
SO WORTHY TO ME
I RECEIVE HIS LOVE
SO GRCIOUSLY
WHEN I LOOK INTO HIS EYES
A DEEPNESS I FIND
THAT EXPLORES HIS HEART
HIS BODY, SOUL AND MIND
SO SPECIAL AND UNIQUE
IN THE MOST GIFTED WAY
HE PRAISES THE LORD
EACH AND EVERY DAY
HOW BLESSED I AM
TO HAVE SOMEONE SO SWEET
WHEN I GET COLD
HE EVEN TURNS UP THE HEAT
WHAT MORE COULD IT BE
OF THIS MAN SO RARE
A SPIRIT SO TRUE
WITH SO MUCH LOVE TO SHARE

71)
FAIRY TALE LOVE

HELLO MY LOVE
IT'S SO VERY HARD TO SLEEP
THE LOVE IN MY HEART
CONTINUES TO CREEP
I LAY ALONE IN MY BED
THIS FEELING I CAN'T SHAKE
I YEARN FOR YOUR LOVE
YOUR BREATH I WANT TO TAKE
SOFTLY I HEAR YOUR VOICE
WHISPERING IN MY EAR
THE BEAUTIFUL WORDS OF LOVE
THAT MAKE MY HEART SHED A TEAR
HOW CAN YOU DO
SUCH A POWERFUL THING TO ME
IS THIS FOR REAL
OR IS IT MAKE BELIEVE
COME INTO ME LOVE
COME INTO ME DEEP
BECAUSE THE LOVE IN MY HEART
FOR YOU CONTINUES TO CREEP

72)
LEADERSHIP

YOU'RE A KEY VALUE
WHEN EVERYTHING SEEMS UNFAIR
IT'S THE BRIDGE OF COMMUNICATION
A SPECIAL WAY TO CARE
YOU'RE A BUILDING OF TRUST
THE TRUTH NEEDS NO DEFENDING
THE LOYALTY OF YOUR NATURE
IS LIMITLESS AND NEVER ENDING
YOU OFFER SO MUCH UNDERSTANDING
WITH A DEEP MEANS OF CONCERN
IT HOLDS STRENGTH AND SECURITY
NEVER HESITATES TO LEARN
YOU SHINE WITH SOMETHING PURE
SOMEONE WHO IS ALWAYS THERE
IT IS A JOY AND HAPPINESS GIVEN
WITH MANY THINGS TO SHARE
YOU'RE A TRUE BLESSING
OF A GIFT SO REAL
I SAY IT WITH ALL HONESTY
THAT IN YOUR LEADERSHIP THESE THINGS I FEEL

73)
HE'S NEVER HARD TO FIND

I'VE TORN DOWN A LOT OF THINGS
TO BUILD A LOT OF NEW THINGS UP
NOW I HAVE AN OVERFLOW
AND NOT A BIG ENOUGH CUP
THE LORD HAS BEEN SO GOOD TO ME
WITH HIS PATIENCE IN EVERY WAY
HE CHESTISES ME, SHOWS ME MERCY
AND GIVES LOVE EVERYDAY
I WILL ALWAYS GIVE MY ALL
TO DO WHAT IS RIGHT
I'VE RECEIVED MANY BLESSINGS
TO BE STANDING IN THE LIGHT
I KNOW I'M NOT PERFECT
BECAUSE THE WORLD IS FULL OF SIN
BUT AS LONG AS I HAVE JESUS
I KNOW I'M GOING TO WIN
SO I PRAY FOR THE UNBELIEVERS
THE UNCONSCIOUS AND BLIND
THAT THEY WILL SEEK THE SALVATION
IN BODY SOUL AND MIND
BECAUSE HE'S NEVER
HARD TO FIND

74)
LORD I'M HURTING

YES LORD I HURT
THE PAIN IS DEEP
I FEEL THAT THE MOUNTAINS
ARE SO STEEP
I CAN'T SEEM TO STAND
PLEASE DEAR LORD
TAKE MY HAND
I CAN'T SEEM TO FIND MY WAY
FOR ME THE SUN IS NOT SHINNING TODAY
I KNOW YOUR THERE
I'VE FELT YOUR PRESENCE NEAR
BUT NOW MY LORD, MY HEART
IS CRIPPLED WITH FEAR
LORD, HELP THE SUN TO SHINE
TO KNOW THAT YOU ARE MINE
HEAL THIS PAIN I FEEL
MAKE YOUR PRESENCE VERY REAL
TODAY, LORD
I GIVE YOU MY ALL
HELP ME DEAR LORD
NOT TO FALL
HOLD ME TIGHT SO I CAN FEEL
WITH ALL YOUR MIGHT
LET PEACE BE STILL

75)
MY BROTHERS

MY BROTHERS COME TO REALIZE
THAT TODAY YOU'RE FREE
THE ONLY PAIN THAT IS CAUSED
IS CREATED MENTALLY
YOU HAVE THE POWER TO WIN
GODS SPIRIT IS IN YOUR HEART
IT'S THE GIFT OF NATURAL FAITH
TO BELIEVE AND NEVER PART
TO VALUE ALL OF THE GLORY
IS TO CONQUER YOUR GREATEST DREAMS
TO WALK WITH THE DEFINITION
FOR UNDEDRSTANDING WHAT IT MEANS
YOU HAVE IT ALL BEFORE YOU
TO BEHOLD THE TRUTH BY RIGHT
IT'S YOUR FUTURE AND YOUR DESTINY
THAT'S WAITING IN THE LIGHT

76)
TENDER LOVE AND CARE

SO SWEET WARM AND TENDER
WITH SO MUCH TO EXPLORE
REMEMBER THE ONE WHO LOVES YOU
AND THE BLESSINGS HE HOLDS IN STORE
WHENEVER YOU GET THE FEELING
TO SHARE WHAT IS IN YOUR HEART
GIVE INTO THE HIGHER SPIRIT
FOR HIS POWER WILL NEVER PART
I LOVE YOU IN SO MANY WAYS
I'M DADDY I'LL ALWAYS CARE
I'LL LEAD YOU TO THE HIGHER SPIRIT
WHO WILL HELP YOU IN ALL AFFAIRS
I CAN ONLY SAY WHAT I FEEL
YOU'RE SO BEAUTIFUL AND SWEET
EVERY MOMENT I THINK OF YOU
MAKES MY LIFE FULL AND COMPLETE

77)
HOT FLASH

DRIFTING AWAY LIKE A CLOUD
A HEART MADE OF STONE
I'VE LOST COMPLETE DIRECTION
HURT AND ALL ALONE
HIDDING BEHIND THE SHADOWS
WAITING IN ORDER OF TURN
AS THE HEAT BEGINS TO BUILD UP
MY SKIN BEGINS TO BURN
CRYING WITH AGONY FOR MERCY
BUT THE CALL REMAINS UNHEARD
BREAKING DOWN TO MY KNEES
BECAUSE NO ONE HAS HEARD A WORD
REACHING MY FINAL DESTINATION
I TRY TO FIGHT ONE MORE TIME
BUT A VOICE FROM OUT OF THE DARKNESS
SAID BE QUIET YOUR SOUL IS MINE

78)
THE CASTLE OF BRICKS

THE CASTLE OF BRICKS
SURROUNDED BY RAZOR WIRE
PROSECUTERS AND JUDGES
CONSTANTLY SPITTING FIRE
INNOCENT OR GUILTY
THE RECORDS STATE THE CRIME
OF THOSE WHO HAVE TO ACCEPT
THE PUNSIHMENT THE TIME
HERE THERE'S NO LOVE
NOT FOR YOU OR FOR ME
EVERYTHING ON THE OUTSIDE
YOU CAN NO LONGER SEE
THOSE WHO SAID THEY LOVE YOU
AFTER A WHILE IT'S HARD TO TELL
THE PHONE CALLS ARE LIMITED
AND SO IS THE MAIL
NOW YOU'RE ON YOUR OWN
THE PAST YOU PUT BEHIND
TO ESTABLISH A NEW LIFE
AND SEASON YOUR MIND
ONE THING IS FOR SURE
THIS WILL BREAK OR MAKE A MAN
CHANGING HIS WHOLE LIFE
TO DETERMINE HOW HE WILL STAND

79)
STAND STRONG

TOGETHER WE STAND
DIVIDED WE FALL
IT'S THE RIGHTEOUS IN HEART
WHO FOREVER STANDS TALL
WITHOUT STEREOTYPING RACES
THE REASONS TO DISCRIMINATE
THOSE WHO ARE INNOCENT
BECAUSE OF IGNORANCE AND HATE
HAND IN HAND WE WALK
IN SEARCH FOR PEACE OF MIND
THOSE WHO CAN SEE
WILL LEAD THE BLIND
NOW WE'RE WEAPONS
IN THIS NEW AGE OF TIME
FROM THE KNOWLEDGE THAT WE'VE GAINED
THAT WAS ONCE CONSIDERED A CRIME
NO MORE PHYSICAL SLAVERY
NOT IN THIS DAY AND AGE
IT'S NOW A MENTAL ASPECT
A WHOLE DIFFERENT PAGE
FOR WHEN THE BODY LIES DOWN
SOULS WILL BE FREE
TO RECEIVE THE REWARD
OF LIFE ETERNALLY

80)
ONE TIME ONLY

IT'S BEEN A LONG TIME
MY BODY IS GETTING WEAK
IT'S KIND OF HARD TO TELL
WHAT I'LL DO WITH A FREAK
NEVER A GIVEN MOMENT
I'LL PROBABLY BEAT HER THERE
IT MIGHT BE A HARSH THING TO SAY
BUT I'LL HAVE HER FEET IN THE AIR
STROKING IN MOTION
POUNDING WITHOUT A CARE
WHEN IT'S ALL OVER
SHE'LL PROBABLY SAY IT WASN'T FAIR
BUT TO KEEP THINGS DOWN
FROM CATCHING A LABEL
I'LL GIVE HER WHAT SHE EARNED
LEAVING THE MONEY ON THE TABLE
WEAK AND DROWSY
SWEAT DRIPPING TO THE GROUND
I'M LEAVING HER HOME
WITHOUT MAKING A SOUND

81)
IT'S NO SECRET

WE ALL GET A LITTLE LONLEY
HEARTS BEGIN TO CRY
FOR DESIRES BEYOND MEASUREMENT
OFTEN WONDERING WHY
WE FIGHT TO REACH OUR DESTINY
THROUGH TRIALS AND TRIBULATIONS
FALLING INTO CHALLENGES
FOR BEARING SITUATIONS
WE ALL HAVE A HIDDEN TALENT
IN STORE AND WILLING TO SHINE
THE LOVE TO SHARE WITH ANOTHER
TO SMOOTH A SURFACE FINE
WE ALL HAVE TO FACE REALITY
EVEN THOUGH IT MAY SEEM UNFAIR
IT'S THE VALUES TO ONLY BEHOLD
TO REMEMBER ALL THAT IS THERE
WE ALL GO THROUGH MUCH SUFFERING
CERTAIN THINGS WE DREAD
BUT IT'S NO SECRET
THAT TEMPTATION LIES AHEAD
IT'S TRULY UP TO YOU
WHERE YOU GO AND HOW FAR
CAUSE YOUR FACE IS IN THE SKY
AS ANOTHER SHINNING STAR

82)
YOU BROKE THE MOLD

THERE'S SOMETHING VERY SPECIAL
ABOUT BEING ONE OF A KIND
THE BEAUTY OF YOUR ATTRACTION
JUST BLOWS MY MIND
YOU'RE MOST TRULY DIFFERENT
THE WAY YOU SHINE ON CLOUDY DAYS
MAKES ME FEEL SO ALIVE
FROM YOUR PLEASURE OF MANY WAYS
IT'S SUCH A BLESSING
A STORY TO BE TOLD
THAT WHEN YOU WERE CREATED
YOU TRULY BROKE THE MOLD
FROM THE DEEPEST OF MY DESIRE
YOUR HEART I'LL ALWAYS PROTECT
AND GIVE YOU THE MOST HIGH
OF LOYALTY, LOVE AND RESPECT
OUT OF ALL THAT I FEEL FOR YOU
MY HEART CAN FINALLY REST
BECAUSE NOTHING IS MORE BEAUTIFUL
THAN HAVING THE BEST

83)
IT'S NOT ABOUT YOU—
IT'S ABOUT THEM

WHEN PEOPLE TALK ABOUT OTHERS
THEY, HER AND HIM
CONSIDER THE SOURCE IN WHICH IT'S FROM
CAUSE IT'S USUALLY ABOUT THEM
EVERYTHING NEED ITS OWN ENERGY
IN WHICH TO FEED
SOME TAKE KINDNESS FOR WEAKNESS
OTHERS ARE SPITEFUL FOR GREED
THESE ARE THE SAME PEOPLE
WHO CLAIM TO LOVE YOU
SMILING WITH FALSE INTENSIONS
MISERY LOVES COMPANY TOO
THEY PRY THEIR WAY INTO YOUR LIFE
WITH CONFIDENCE AND MUNIPULATION
DESTROYING EVERYTHING IN THEIR PATH
WITH RUTHLESS PERPETRATION
THE SAD PART ABOUT IT ALL
IS THAT THEY DON'T HAVE A CLUE
THEY'RE THERE OWN WORSE ENEMY
AND IT HAS NOTHING TO DO WITH YOU

84)
HOME SICK

VISIONS OF MY FAMILY
FLASH IN MY HEAD
OF HOW WE PRAY TOGETHER
EVEN BROKE BREAD
THE VOICES OF THE CHILDREN
RING LOUD IN MY EARS
THE VISION OF SMILING FACES
BRINGS ME MANY TEARS
WITH A DEEP FELT LONGING
TO GET BACK TO LIFE
I FEEL THE PAIN OF SEPARATION
I REALLY MISS MY WIFE
IT'S SOMETHING ABOUT THE UNITY
THAT MAKES A FAMILY GROW
IF I COULD ONLY BE THERE
THE MORE LOVE I WILL SHOW
I MISS LOOKING IN THERE EYES
SAYING EVERYTHING IS ALRIGHT
NOW I HAVE TO TELL MYSELF
CAUSE I'M HOME SICK TONIGHT

85)
MYSTIFYING

RUNNING ALL THROUGH MY MIND
ALL THROUGH MY HEART
AN EVERLASTING FEELING
THAT WILL NEVER EVER PART
WITH SO MUCH LOVE
A HEART FILLED TO INSPIRE
YOU'RE THE ONLY WOMAN
THAT I TRULY DESISRE
MY DAYS AND NIGHTS
YOU HAVE FOUND A WAY TO SOOTH
THE TENDER TOUCH OF YOUR LOVE
IS INTENSE AND SMOOTH
CRAWLING THROUGH MY SYSTEM
IN MY HEART, TO THE CORE
MARINATING IS A LOVE
THAT I'VE NEVER FELT BEFORE

86)
DROWNING IN
MY DESIRE FOR YOU

MANY NIGHTS I LAY AWAKE
DEEPLY CONTEPLATING BEFORE I SLEEP
ABOUT THE LOVE I FEEL FOR YOU
I SO LONG TO KEEP
THE INSPIRATION ONLY ENHANCES
AS MY EMOTIONS TAKE CONTROL
LIKE A FREE SPIRIT IN THE WIND
I LET MY FEELINGS FLOW
I WANT TO FEEL YOUR LOVE
AND THE TEXTURE OF YOUR SKIN
SMELL THE SCENT OF YOUR HAIR
FEEL THE MOISTURE WITHIN
IF I COULD BE WITH YOU NOW
IT WOULD BE A DREAM COME TRUE
I WILL GIVE YOU ALL OF MY HEART
CAUSE I'M DROWING IN LOVE TO BE WITH YOU

87)
AGAINST THE GRAIN

YOU CAN'T LOVE
IF YOU HARBOR HATE
YOU CAN'T BE ON TIME
IF YOU'RE ALWAYS LATE
YOU CAN'T ALWAYS HAVE
THINGS YOUR WAY
BECAUSE THE SUN STILL SHINES
EVEN ON A CLOUDY DAY
IF YOU SAY YOU ARE MY FRIEND
THAN DON'T TALK BEHIND MY BACK
BECAUSE YOU MIGHT FIND YOURSELF
WALKING THE SAME TRACK
ALTHOUGH YOU MAY WANT
YOUR CAKE AND EAT IT TOO!
YOU ALSO MUST REMEMBER
THE WORLD DOESN'T REVOLVE AROUND YOU!
DON'T SAY YOU HAVE LOVE
IF IT'S NOT IN YOUR HEART
AND DON'T PLAY A ROLE
THAT IS NOT YOUR PART.

88)
A SLAVE IN MY OWN HOME

IT'S THE MOST DEPRESSING FEELING
A MENTAL FORM OF ABUSE
MY KINDNESS IS TAKEN FOR WEAKNESS
FOR OTHER BENEFITS OR PERSONAL USE
TRYING MY BEST TO STAY SPIRITUALLY STRONG
I'M PRAISED FOR WHAT I CAN DO GOOD
AS FAR AS APPRECIATION AND RESPECT
I MIGHT AS WELL BE A STICK OF WOOD
OUT OF MY WAY AND BEYOND MY MEANS
TO BUILD SOMETHING THEY NEVER HAD
SPIRTUALLY, LOVE AND STRUCTURE
YOU WOULD THINK THEY WOULD BE GLAD
WHEN I SPEAK ON APPRECIATON
ALL THE THINGS TO BE THANKFUL FOR
I GET CROSSED EYES WORDS THAT SPIT FIRE
EVIL THOUGHTS AND A SLAMMED DOOR
NO ONE CAN EVER IMAGINE
HOW THIS REALLY FEELS TO ME
A TRUE MAN OF LOVE, MORALS AND VALUES
THEY CAN'T EVEN SEE
I DON'T CLAIM TO BE AN ANGEL
I MYSELF CAN BE WRONG
BUT I'M FAR FROM BEING BLIND
I'M A VICTIM BECAUSE I'M STRONG
WHAT I DO DOESN'T REALLY SEEM TO MATTER
UNLESS IT'S GOING THEIR WAY
I'M BEING DRAINED OF MY PEACE
AND AT TIMES I DON'T EVEN PRAY
I'M SCARED AND SO FULL OF FEAR

FOR LESS I'VE SEEN MANY LIVES SOLD
IF I DON'T PRY AWAY FROM THIS MADNESS
EVEN MY HEART WILL BECOME COLD
SIGNS AND SYMBOLS SPIRITUALLY IN LINE
WILL ALWAYS DIRECT A FOCUSED MIND
WHILE THE PHYSICAL WORLD OF COMPREHENDING
WILL SEARCH BUT CAN NOT FIND
A SLAVE IN MY OWN HOME
AS I CONTINUE TO BE
MY LOVE, MY CARE, MY CONCERN
A REAL MAN THEY CAN NOT SEE

89)
THE VALUE OF SMALL THINGS

ARE SOMETIMES CROSSED UP
FROM FINANCIAL AMOUNTS
IT'S NOT HOW MUCH IT COSTS
IT'S THE THOUGHT THAT COUNTS
IT COULD BE SOMETHING
THAT YOU CAN BARELY SEE
THE SPECIAL PART ABOUT IT
IS THAT IT CAME FROM ME
SOMETHING AS SMALL AS A TEAR
THAT IS JUST ABOUT TO FALL
CAN EASILY BE EVAPORATED
BY A SIMPLE PHONE CALL
WHAT MIGHT NOT BE OF A VALUE TO YOU
IS A DEEP VALUE TO ME
BECAUSE THE VALUE OF SMALL THINGS
IS HOW BIG THINGS COME TO BE

90)
IT REALLY DOESN'T MATTER

IT REALLY DOESN'T MATTER
WHAT YOU HAVE OR WHAT YOU GOT
I HAVE A FRIEND THAT I CAN COUNT ON
WEATHER YOU ARE THERE OR NOT
IT REALLY DOESN'T MATTER
IF YOU DON'T APPRECAITE ME
IT'S BECAUSE OF YOUR OWN BLINDNESS
WHY YOU'RE NOT FREE
IT REALLY DOESN'T MATTER
IF YOU DON'T RESPECT MY LOVE
BECAUSE MY TRUST IS IN MUCH GREATER
BEYOND, AND ABOVE
IT REALLY DOESN'T MATTER
ABOUT WHAT YOU TRY TO HIDE
BECAUSE WHEN YOU LOOK FOR ME
I'LL BE ON THE OTHER SIDE

91)
LIFE GOES ON

LIKE THE ROTATION OF THE WORLD
TIME WAITS FOR NO ONE
HERE TODAY, GONE TOMORROW
LIFE IS DONE
SOMETHINGS HAVE TO DIE
SO OTHER THINGS CAN LIVE
NOTHING IS BY ACCIDENT
SOMETHING GOT TO GIVE
WHAT GOES AROUND COMES AROUND
AND WHAT IS LOST SOMETIMES COMES BACK
SOMETHINGS ARE OFF COURSE
WHILE OTHERS ARE ON TRACK
EVERYTHING THAT GOES UP
WILL EVENTUALLY COME DOWN
EVERY KING AND EVERY QUEEN
WILL SOON LOOSE THEIR CROWN
ON A TEMPORARY STATUS
FOR EVERYTHING UNDER THE SUN
TIME WAITS FOR NO ONE
NO PLACE TO HIDE, NO PLACE TO RUN

92)
HONEY IT'S YOU

HONEY IT'S YOU
I SEE AROUND AND ABOUT ME
HONEY IT'S YOU
WHEN LIFE REACHES MATURITY
HONEY IT'S YOU
BEING LOVING SWEET AND KIND
WHEN DISTANCE IS BETWEEN US
YOU ARE ALWAYS ON MY MIND
HONEY IT'S YOU
THAT MAKES MY RISING A PART OF CHANGE
HONEY IT'S YOU
THAT MAKES ME FEEL STRANGE
HONEY IT'S YOU
WITHIN EVERY STROKE
HONEY IT'S YOU
A LOT OF MY SELFISH WAYS I BROKE
HONEY IT'S YOU
THAT MAKES LIFE WORTH WHILE
HONEY IT'S YOU
THAT GAVE ME A NEW STYLE

93)
ONE CALL, ONE WAY

IN THIS BOOK
THERE'S DEEP INSPIRATIONS
THE FACTS OF REALITY
DREAMS AND SITUATIONS
I'VE TRULY BEEN BLESSED
WITH A STRONG POSITIVE DRIVE
I GIVE MY ALL TO OTHERS
ABOUT WHAT REALLY KEEPS ME ALIVE
IT'S ALL ABOUT WHAT YOU FEEL
NO SECRETS, NO LIES
WITHOUT THE COVERS OF DARKNESS
NO MASK, NO DISQUISE
I WRITE OF FULL CONSCIOUSNESS
OF ALL THAT I CAN SHARE
GIVING A MESSAGE TO BUILD
BECAUSE IT'S TIME TO BE AWARE
LIFE IS ONLY TEMPORARY
SO BE READY FOR THE DRILL
BECAUSE THE CALL IS ABOUT TO BE MADE
BY THE POWER OF GODS WILL

94)
STARS ALWAYS SHINE

OUT OF ALL THE THINGS I'VE BEEN THROUGH
NO WORDS COULD EVER DESCRIBE
THE REASONS FOR MY SUFFERING
THE PAIN THAT I CRY
I'VE COME TO FIND WITHIN MYSELF
A SENSE OF INNER PEACE
TO GUIDE ME THROUGH THIS JOURNEY
FOR THE TRUTH I WILL RELEASE
I KNOW THAT I WILL BE CHALLENGED
BY THE TEMPTATIONS OF THE FLAME
I WILL NEVER HOLD IT AGAINST ANOTHER
TO FIND FAULT OR BLAME
I KNOW THAT I HAVE A CHOICE
MY DESTINY TO MAKE OR MASTER
TO BE CAUTIOUSLY AWARE
OF CONSEQUENCES AND DISASTER
A POSITIVE AND PRODUCTIVE IMAGE
I WILL ALWAYS TRY TO INSPIRE
THAT ANYTHING CAN BE ACCOMPLISHED
BASED ON WHAT YOU DESIRE
ON THIS DAY I SINCERELY HONOR
A LIGHT SO TRULY DEVINE
CAUSE THE GIFT OF ETERNAL LIFE
IS IN THE ONE WHO WILL ALWAYS SHINE

95)
HELLO BABY

LETS DO THE RIGHT THINGS
SO LISTEN TO MY HEART AS I SAY
I WILL ALWAYS LOVE YOU
IN THE MOST GRACIOUS WAY
PLEASE UNDERSTAND
BELIEVE IN ME
WHEN I SAY I LOVE YOU
IT COMES WITH A GUARANTEE
FOR ALL YOU EVER DESIRE
ANYTHING THAT YOU NEED
DEEP WITHIN MY HEART
I HOLD THE KEY
GIVING ALL OF ME TO YOU
A PLEASURE TO SATISFY
A DEEPNESS WITHIN
THAT WILL NEVER RUN DRY
HELLO BABY
LETS DO THE RIGHT THINGS
FOR THE BLESSINGS OF HAPPINESS
AND FOR ALL THAT LOVE BRINGS

96)
WHENEVER, CALL ON ME

WHEN YOUR HEART IS FEELING LONELY
NEEDING SOMEONE TO BE THERE
YOU CAN ALWAYS CALL ON ME
I WILL STROKE YOU WITH CARE
WHEN YOUR BODY IS SO WEAK
YOU CAN CALL ON ME
I'LL BE YOUR ENERGY FREAK
WHENEVER YOU WANT TO TALK
OR MAYBE SHED A FEW TEARS
YOU CAN ALWAYS CALL ON ME
TO WIPE YOUR EYES WITH OPEN EARS
WHENEVER YOU ARE FEELING HURT
IN NEED OF RESPECT
YOU CAN ALWAYS CALL ON ME
I WILL LOVE AND PROTECT
WHENEVER YOU ARE FEELING SAD
AND YOUR HEART IS FEELING FROZE
YOU CAN ALWAYS CALL ON ME
TO WARM YOU WITH A SMILE AND A ROSE

97)
DON'T BLAME ME

DON'T BLAME ME
FOR WHAT YOU'VE DONE
ALTHOUGH IT'S NO FUN
WHEN THE RABBIT HAS THE GUN
DON'T BLAME ME
FOR THE WAY YOUR LIFE HAS BEEN
CAUSE YOU'VE HAD OPPORTUNITIES
AND CHANCES TO WIN
DON'T BLAME ME
FOR REASONS TO MAKE OTHER PLANS
CAUSE THIS IS ABOUT YOU
I'VE WASHED MY HANDS
DON'T BLAME ME
TO GO AND VENT OUT
OF ALL THE NEGATIVE THINGS
THAT I'VE BEEN ABOUT
DON'T BLAME ME
FOR YOUR OWN MISTAKE
CAUSE I'M NOT YOUR ENEMY
IT'S YOU THAT YOU HATE

98)
I LOVE YOU JESUS

I LOVE YOU JESUS
I LOVE YOU JESUS
I LOVE YOU JESUS
I LOVE YOU JESUS
I LOVE YOU JESUS
I LOVE YOU JESUS
I LOVE YOU JESUS
I LOVE YOU JESUS
I LOVE YOU JESUS
I LOVE YOU JESUS
I LOVE YOU JESUS
I LOVE YOU JESUS
I LOVE YOU JESUS
I LOVE YOU JESUS
I LOVE YOU JESUS
I LOVE YOU JESUS   *I LOVE YOU JESUS*
I LOVE YOU JESUS   *I LOVE YOU JESUS*
I LOVE YOUU JESUS   *I LOVE YOU JESUS*
I LOVE YOU JESUS   *I LOVE YOU JESUS*
I LOVE YOU JESUS   *I LOVE YOU JESUS*
I LOVE YOU JESUS, I LOVE YOU JESUS

99)
A KING AND A QUEEN

TOGETHER THEY SHARE A THRONE
POLISHING EACH OTHER CROWNS
SUPPORTING ONE ANOTHER FULLY
THROUGH UPS AND DOWNS
PEOPLE FROM ALL AROUND
TALK ABOUT THEIR SHINE
THEIR SWORDS WITH EDGES
THAT CUT SO FINE
WITH A DEEP RESPECT
THEY TREAT EVERYONE FAIR
THEY HAVE THE GIFT OF LOVE
TO APPRECIATE AND CARE
BY THE LAW OF RIGHTIOUSNESS
THEY WILL ALWAYS PROJECT
AN UNCONDITIONAL LOVE
TO REACH OUT AND PROTECT
TOGETHER THIS KING AND QUEEN
WILL BE A STORY FOR LIFE
EDWARD & KATHY MCGILL
HUSBAND AND WIFE

100)
TALK TO MY QUEEN

I WANT TO KNOW WHAT'S IN YOUR HEART
FOR WHATEVER IT MAY MEAN
YOU'RE THE BLESSING I'VE BEEN LOOKING FOR
IN THE MIST OF MY DREAM
I WANT TO FEEL YOUR BEAUTY
AS I LOOK INTO YOUR EYES
FEELING A VIBRATION OF LOVE
WITH NO HIDDEN DISQUISE
I WANT TO WHISPER SOFTLY
THESE PRECIOUS WORDS IN YOUR EAR
I LOVE YOU MY QUEEN
FOR THERE IS NOTHING TO FEAR
LOVE IS LIKE THE WIND
A FREE SILKY RIDE
I WANT TO SPEND MY LIFE WITH YOU
IN ETERNITY, ON THE OTHER SIDE
I WANT TO GIVE YOU MY LOVE
MY HEART COMES COMPLETE
LIKE A DREAM WORTH LIVING
A SOFT DEEP SLEEP
LET ME TAKE YOU TO THAT PLACE
I GIVE MY ALL TO SACRAFICE
TO SEE YOU HAPPILY IN LOVE
IN THE LAND OF PARADISE
I LOVE YOU MY QUEEN
WITH ALL OF MY HEART
I PROMISE YOU A DEVOTION
THAT WILL NEVER EVER PART

101)
FORGIVE ME

PLEASE FORGIVE ME MY LORD
OF BEING OUT OF TOUCH
YOU KNOW DEEP IN MY HEART
I LOVE YOU SO MUCH
ENSNARED BY THE WORLDS DESIRES
MY SPIRITUAL DUTY HAS BECOME LOW
I FEEL MYSELF SLIPPING AWAY
LOOSING MY GLOW
I TAKE FULL OWNERSHIP
FOR ALL THAT I'VE DONE
IN GREAT HOPES TO GET IT RIGHT
AND WITH YOU BECOME ONE
PLEASE FORGIVE ME LORD
FOR GOING ASTRAY
I'M ON MY HANDS AND KNEES PRAYING
FOR YOU TO LEAD THE WAY

102)
OUR NATURE

NATURE HAS GIVEN US MUCH
ANIMALS, FLOWERS AND TREES
THE TEXURE OF SWEET POLLEN
THE BIRDS AND THE BEES
THE AIR THAT WE BREATH
WATERS THAT STRETCH FOR MILES
AND ALL OF THIS IS RECORDED
IN THE CREATIVE HEAVENLY FILES
A SUN SO BRIGHT
A WARMTH THAT FLOWS
A MOON WITH LIGHT
AT NIGHT IT GLOWS
FROM THE SPARK OF A TWINKLING STAR
TO THE CLOUDS THAT CROSS THE SKYS
WHEN I LOOK AT NATURE
I SEE THE SAME THINGS IN YOUR EYES
MY WISH IS FOR
THIS LIFE TO REMAIN NEW
BLESSING ME WITH THE BEAUTY OF NATURE
AND SOMEONE SPECIAL LIKE YOU

103)
STAYING ON MY MIND

24-7 I CAN'T HELP THE WAY I FEEL
IT'S YOU AND YOUR LOVE
YOUR VIBRATION
THE WAY YOU SHOW CONCERN
WITH SUCH APPRECIATION
52 WEEKS
I CAN'T HELP THE WAY I FEEL
IT'S YOU AND YOUR LOVE
YOUR SPIRIT I CAN'T IGNORE
A PASSIONATE LOVE THAT ALWAYS LEAVES ME CRAVING
AND CRYING FOR MORE
365 I CAN'T HELP THE WAY I FEEL
I HAVE ONLY COME TO REALIZE
THAT THIS FEELING IS GOING TO LAST FOREVER
AS FOR ANY DOUBTS OR REGRETS
O' NO BABY" NEVER, NEVER
DARLING
THE STIMULATION OF YOUR LOVE
IS WHAT REALLY KEEPS ME ALIVE
A ROTATION OF TRUE ECSTASY
A DESTINY, A CREATIVE DRIVE
A TRUE LOVE
IS SO HARD TO FIND
MISSING YOU IS DOING DAMAGE
TO MY HEART, TO MY MIND

104)
JESUS HAS HIS OWN PRIVATE LINE

THERE COMES A TIME IN LIFE
WHEN THE FAMILY STARTS TO SEPARATE
WITH FAITH THERE'S NO NEED TO WORRY
CAUSE WE WILL COME TOGETHER AGAIN
AT GODS GOLDEN GATE
JESUS IS ALWAYS THERE FOR US FROM THE BEGINNING TO
THE END
NO MATTER WHAT FATE WE MAY FACE
HE WILL ALWAYS BE OUR BEST FRIEND
FAITH AND THE POWER OF SPRIT
IS WHAT KEEPS US ALIVE
THE UNDERSTANDING OF HIS WORDS
GIVES US THAT POSITIVE DRIVE
YOU DON'T NEED A DIME
THE CALL IS FREE
ALL YOU NEED TO HAVE
IS FAITH AND BELIEVE
NO APPOINTMENT NECESSARY
ANYTIME IS FINE
HE'S HANDING OUT BLESSINGS
I FINALLY GOT MINE
SO MAKE THE CALL
DON'T BE AFRAID
FOR HIS RIGHTIOUS WILL SHOW
ON JUDGEMENT DAY

105)
DO THE RIGHT THING

DO WHAT IS RIGHT
THEN YOU SHALL NOT FAIL
FOLLOW WHAT IS IN YOUR HEART
YOUR LIFE WILL SAIL
FOR THE TRUTH NEEDS NO DEFENDING
YOU'LL NEVER HAVE TO LOOK BACK
CAUSE YOU'VE DONE ALL THE RIGHT THINGS
TO KEEP YOUR LIFE ON TRACK
WE ARE THE MAKERS AND MASTERS
OF OUR OWN DESTINIES
WE'VE BEEN TRULY BLESSED
WITH UNLIMITED POSSIBILITIES
DO WHAT YOU FEEL IS RIGHT
NEVER ACT BEFORE YOU THINK
WHEN YOU LOOSE FOCUS
YOUR LIFE WILL SINK
REMEMBER TO STAY CONSCIOUS
EXERCISE YOUR DRIVE
BECAUSE LIFE IS TOO SHORT
TO BE AWARE IS TOO BE ALIVE

106)
A PROVERB

THE LORD IS MY GUIDE
WISDOM IS MY CROWN
MY FAITH IS IN THE LORD
KEEPS MY BACK OFF THE GROUND
KNOWLEDGE IS MY KEY
FOR DIRECTION I UNDERSTAND
I LISTEN CAREFULLY TO THE WORDS
THAT GIVE ME THE ULTIMATE COMMAND
WITH HONESTY I SPEAK
THE LORD IS MY FRIEND
THE TRUTH HOLDS HONOR
NEEDS NO-ONE TO DEFEND
MY HEART CAN SEE
WHAT MY EYES CANNOT
THE LORD REMEMBERS THE THINGS
THAT I'VE FORGOT
IT'S A MIRACLE TO HAVE THE BEAUTY
OF SUCH A LIFE TO LIVE
BLESSED WITH A CROWN
A HEART TO GIVE
WHY AM I WORTHY
OF SUCH A POWERFUL THING
I BELIEVE IN THE MESSAGE
THAT THE LORD CAME TO BRING

107)
THE BLOOD

GOOD MORNING MY LORD
THANKYOU FOR A NEW DAY
I NEED YOU IN MY LIFE
SO LORD PLEASE STAY
WHATEVER I MAY ENCOUNTER
FROM THIS MOMENT OUT
LET IT BE AUTHROIZED BY YOU
MY FAITH HAS NO DOUBT
LET THE BLOOD OF YOUR HOLINESS
RAIN DOWN ON ME TODAY
LEADING ME BY RIGHTEOUSNESS
DELIVERING ME IN EVERY WAY
SHIELD ME WITH THE ARMOUR
AGAINST THE WICKED THAT LIES
WITHIN THE ATMOSPHERE
DELIVER ME FROM SIN
TURN UP THE VOLUME SO THAT I CAN HEAR
I CAN'T DO THIS ON MY OWN
O'LORD I DO BELIEVE
THAT BY YOUR BLOOD
THERE IS NOTHING I CAN'T ACHIEVE

108)
TOUCH ME O'LORD

TOUCH ME IN THE MORNING
TOUCH ME ATNIGHT
TOUCH ME IN SUCH A WAY
THAT I CAN BE THE LIGHT
THANKYOU FOR YOUR LOVE
THE BLESSINGS GIVEN TO ME
ONCE I WAS BLIND
NOW I CAN SEE
I CALL ON YOU
YOUR BLOOD I CRAVE
YOU'RE THE ONLY ONE
WHO CAN HEAL AND SAVE
I KNOW THAT I'M A SINNER
IN YOU I TRULY BELIEVE
THAT YOU ARE MY SALVATION
THE ONLY WAY TO BE FREE
TOUCH ME IN THE MORNING
TOUCH ME AT NIGHT
TOUCH ME IN SUCH A WAY
THAT I CAN BE LIGHT

109)
HERE TODAY &
GONE TOMORROW

NOTHING IS PROMISED
TO ANYONE ON EARTH
CAUSE THE POWER OF SIN
HAS GIVEN ITSELF BIRTH
BLESSED IS THE MAN
WHO PRAISES HIS DAY
CAUSE IN ALL REALITY
IT COULD HAVE WENT THE OTHER WAY
LIVE LIKE YOU'VE NEVER LIVED
BEFORE IN YOUR LIFE
BECAUSE THERE IS ALWAYS PRESSURE
FROM TEMPTATION AND STRIFE
SO LET LIFE BE
A REFLECTION OF YOUR FACE
THIS WILL DETERMINE
YOUR DESTINY AND YOUR PLACE
LIFE IS A MYSTERY
IT COMES AND IT GOES
THE THINGS THAT ARE IN STORE
NOBODY REALLY KNOWS

110)
SEASON GREETINGS

WE LIVE BY THE SEASONS
IN GROWTH WE CHANGE
TO ACCEPT THE PURITIES OF LIFE
THAT ARE WELL ARRANGED
AS WE SHARE LAUGHS AND SMILES
SENDING OUT SPECIAL GIFTS
THAT TRAVEL FOR MILES
MAKING OUR DEDICATIONS
TO THOSE WE LOVE AND MISS
GIVING INTO THE GRACE
OF A HUG OR A KISS
TO SHARE THIS MOMENT WITH YOU
IS A VISION SEEN SO CLEAR
A FEELING OF TRUE WARMTH
OF A HEART SO NEAR
THE NEW YEAR HAS COME
LOVE AND HAPPINESS WE SHARE
SPECIAL THOUGHTS OF CONCERN
TENDER LOVE AND CARE
TO YOU I SEND MY BLESSINGS
I VALUE IN A SPECIAL WAY
HOPING THAT EVERYTHING IS GOING WELL
HAPPY HOLIDAY

111)
THANK YOU DEAR GOD

THANK YOU DEAR GOD
FOR SENDING HIM TO ME
SO FAITHFUL AND STRONG
AND LOVE FOR FAMILY
WHATEVER YOU DID TO HIM
PLEASE DON'T STOP
HE'S FILLED WITH A RICHNESS
THE CREAM OF THE CROP
HE'S DEDICATED AND DEVOTED
A LOVE SO VERY TRUE
TO HIM NOTHING IS IMPOSSIBLE
BECAUSE HE BELIEVES IN YOU
WHAT MORE CAN I ASK FOR
I RESPECT AND APPRECIATE
HIS LOVE FOR ME AND MY FAMILY
THE WAY HE COMMUNICATES
THANK YOU DEAR GOD
FOR BRINGING HIM INTO MY LIFE
THANK YOU DEAR GOD
FOR MAKING ME HIS WIFE

112)
GUILT

I FOUND MYSELF STRUGGLING
DEEP IN MY DARKEST HOUR
RUBBING AGAINST THE GRAIN
LOOSING MY POWER
VOICES IN MY HEAD
I SEEK FOR DIRECTION
SLIPPING WAY OUT BOUNDS
LOOSING PROTECTION
I FIGHT AGAINST THE TEMPTATIONS
FOR EASY WAYS TO GAIN
BUT MY CONSCIOUS IS SPEAKING TRUTH
TO KEEP ME FROM PAIN
AS I CHANGE MY STATE OF MIND
MY GUILT STARTS TO POUR
MY HEART BEGINS TO OVERFLOW
FOR RIGHTIOUSNESS ONCE MORE
OH HOLY AND BEHOLD HE SPEAKS
HE WATCHES OVER ME
PROTECTING ME FROM THE EVIL
KEEPING MY SOUL FREE

113)
YOUR TEARS I STORE

SAFELY IN A BOTTLE
YOUR TEARS I STORE
ALLOW ME TO LOVE YOU
FOREVER AND MORE
YOU'RE THE SWEETNESS
FOR WHOM I DELIGHT
WITH A SMILE SO BEAUTIFUL
A SPIRIT SO BRIGHT
OH LORD GIVE ME THE STRENGTH
FOR A QUEEN SO FINE
CAUSE EVERY GIFT FROM YOU
IS PRECIOUS AND DEVINE
LISTEN MY DEAR
TO THESE WORDS I SPEAK TO YOU
AS THEY COME FROM MY HEART
SINCERELY TRUE
WITH MY DEEPEST COMPASSION
DESIRE TO PLEASE
ALL THE LITTLE THINGS
TO MAKE YOU FEEL AT EASE
WITH A CREATIVE SPIRIT
LOVE FOREVER AND MORE
SAFELY IN A BOTTLE
YOUR TEARS I STORE

114)
FACE THE MIRROR

FACE THE MIRROR
CAUSE IT'S YOU THAT NEEDS TO SEE
THE CRACKS AND WRINKLES
THAT SHOW YOUR MISERY
WHEN I SAID GOOD MORNING
YOU LOOKED AT ME AND FROWNED
AS IF I WAS THE ONE
WHO BROUGHT YOUR LIFE DOWN
THE ONE YOU'RE FIGHTING WITH
IS DEEP WITHIN
IT'S A CURSE OF THE WICKED
AN UNGRATEFUL SIN
AS THE MAKER AND MASTERS
OF OUR OWN DESTINY
THE LORD IS YOUR SALVATION
REPENTENCE IS THE KEY
TO BRING YOU OUT OF YOUR PAIN
OF SO MUCH MISERY
THE NEXT TIME YOU FACE THE MIRROR
A MIRACLE YOU WILL SEE
A HEART OF DILEVERENCE
A SOUL SET FREE

115)
LET ME

LET ME LOVE YOU MY DEAR
RELIEVE YOU OF YOUR STRESS
LET ME ENGRAVE IN YOU
MY LOVE, WITH A PERMANENT ADDRESS
LET ME SHARE WITH YOU
A HAPPINESS THAT COMES FROM ABOVE
LET ME FILL YOUR CUP
FROM THE FAUCET OF MY LOVE
LET ME EMBRACE YOU GENTLY
NOURISH YOUR TENDER HEART
LET ME SHOW YOU COMPASSION
WITH A WILL TO NEVER DEPART
LET ME SHOW YOU A FAITFUL
AND SINCERE UNDERSTANDING
LET ME CARRY YOU DOWN
TO A SOFT AND GENTLE LANDING
LET ME INVEST MY LOVE
IN YOU FOREVER AND MORE
LET ME EXPRESS THIS TRULY
THAT IT'S YOU I ADORE

116)
LETS MAKE LOVE

IN THE MORNING
LATE AT NIGHT
RAIN ON ME
SATISFY MY APPETITE
LET THE EVIDENCE BE
OF HEAT AND SWEAT
A MOMENT TO ALWAYS REMEMBER
WITHOUT ANY REGRET
TALK TO ME SOFTLY
TELL ME HOW YOU FEEL
TOUCH ME GENTLY
BABY JUST KEEP IT REAL
LIKE THE TEXTURE OF CREAM
RISING TO THE TOP
MY DESISRE AWAITS
TO TASTE EVERY SINGLE DROP

117)
A REAL MAN

HE'S THE KIND OF MAN
WHO SHOWS LOVE AND CONCERN
HE'S THE KIND OF MAN
WHO NEVER HESITATES TO LEARN
HE'S THE KIND OF MAN
WHO DOESN'T CREEP AT NIGHT
HE'S THE KIND OF MAN
WHO LEADS BY LIGHT
HE'S THE KIND OF MAN
WHO DOESN'T ARGUE AND FIGHT
HE'S THE KIND OF MAN
WHO LIKES TO KEEP THINGS RIGHT
HE'S THE KIND OF MAN
WHO WILL NOT LIE
HE'S THE KIND OF MAN
FOR HIS FAMILY HE WILL DIE
HE'S THE KIND OF MAN
WHO WORKS HARD FOR MANY DAYS
HE'S THE KIND OF MAN
WHO KNEELS DOWN AND PRAYS

118)
JUST IMAGINE

JUST IMAGINE EVERYONE BEING BLIND
YOU'RE THE ONLY ONE WHO CAN SEE
EVERY DOOR LOCKED
YOU'RE THE ONLY ONE WITH A KEY
JUST IMAGINE IF THE WIND
NEVER BLEW
LIFE AT A STILLNESS
NOTHING NEW
JUST IMAGINE NOT BEING ABLE TO HEAR
OR TALK
NEEDING SOMEONE BY YOUR SIDE
TO HELP YOU WALK
JUST IMAGINE BEING BORN
LEARNING HOW TO CRAWL
BUT SPENDING THE REST OF YOUR LIFE
BEING FED BY A STRAW
JUST IMAGINE NOT BEING ABLE
TO TAKE YOURSELF THERE
JUST IMAGINE HAVING LOVE
BUT WITH NO ONE TO SHARE
JUST IMAGINE YOURSELF
AND ALL THAT YOU GOT
NOW THINK ABOUT OTHERS
WHO SEE A LITTLE AS A LOT

119)
THANK YOU JESUS

FOR YOU HAVE GIVEN ME LIFE
SO MUCH TO LIVE FOR
A SPIRIT THAT LIVES
FOREVER AND MORE
THANK YOU FOR CARRYING ME THROUGH
TRIALS AND TRIBULATIONS
THANK YOU FOR THE DOORS TO ESCAPE
DANGEROUS SITUATIONS
THANK YOU FOR CHESTIZING ME
I KNEW I WAS WRONG
THANK YOU FOR THE WISDOM
TO KEEP ME STRONG
THANK YOU FOR DYING FOR ME
A LIFE I FEEL I DON'T DESERVE
FOR THIS CAUSE I WILL HONOR
YOU LORD I WILL SERVE

120)
LOST BUT FOUND

WASHED AWAY A PRETTY SMILE
FROM TEARS OF PAIN
SHE LOOKS FOR A WAY OUT
BUT IT CONTINUES TO RAIN
A SLAVE FOR THE WORLD
AS THE CLOUDS TAKE PLACE
STRIPPED OF HER IDENITY
AND EVEN HER RACE
NO WHERE TO RUN
NO WHERE TO HIDE
HER MIND STARTS TRIPPING
ABOUT COMMITTING SUICIDE
FLASHES OF HER LIFE
MOVE THROUGH HER HEAD
AS SHE GETS CLOSER AND CLOSER
TO HER DEATH BED
WITH ONE LAST BREATH
SHE CRIES FOR HER LIFE
THE WILL TO OVERCOME
THE PAIN THE STRIFE
AS A STAR SHINNED UPON HER
A SMILE GREW ON HER FACE
HER SOUL IS NOW RESTING
IN A DEVINE AND PEACEFUL PLACE
NO MORE TEARS
NO MORE RAIN
NO MORE DARK CLOUDS
NO MORE PAIN

121)
LOOK WITHIN YOURSELF

DON'T BE TO QUICK
TO JUDGE ANOTHER PERSON WRONG
LOOK WITHIN YOURSELF
CAUSE YOU MAY NOT BE SO STRONG
LIFE IS NOT PERFECT
WE LIVE AND WE LEARN
FOR THOSE WHO JUDGE OTHERS
WILL SOON HAVE A TURN
IT'S A LIFE LONG PROCESS
WE DO WHAT IT TAKES
WE STRUGGLE AND FALL
MAKE MANY MISTAKES
LIFE IS TO BE TAKEN SERIOUSLY
IT'S FAR BEYOND A GAME
IT'S WRITTEN IN THE BOOK OF WISDOM
THAT NONE OF US ARE THE SAME
LOOK WITHIN YOURSELF
BEFORE YOU JUDGE ANOTHER
I WILL ALWAYS LOVE YOU
MY SISTER, MY BROTHER

122)
FIVE COATS OF LOVE

THE FIRST COAT WOULD BE
THE GIFT OF UNDERSTANDING
FOR THE REASONS
THAT ARE DEMANDING
THE SECOND COAT WOULD BE
THE GIFT OF RESPECT
WHICH I'LL ALWAYS CHARISH
LOVE AND PROTECT
THE THIRD COAT WOULD BE
THE GIFT OF APPRECIATION
FOR BUILDING THE STRONGEST
BRIDGE OF COMMUNICATION
THE FOURTH COAT WOULD BE
A DEDICATION OF LOVE
A ARMOR OF SOLITUDE
THAT CAN ONLY COME FROM ABOVE
THE FIFTH COAT WOULD BE
A BLANKET OF SECURITY
AND FOR STRUCTURE
THE BEST OF MY ABILITY

123)
GOOD MORNING

GOOD MORNING MY LOVE
HOW ARE YOU TODAY
JUST A FEW LINES TO SAY
I LOVE YOU IN A SPECIAL WAY
BLESSED ONCE AGAIN
TO SEE YOUR PRETTY FACE
HEARING YOUR SOFT VOICE
BEING IN THE RIGHT PLACE
THERE IS NO OTHER PLACE
I WOULD RATHER BE
RIGHT HERE WITH YOU
MAKING LOVE SO DELICATELY
SO LETS LIVE TODAY
LIKE IT'S OUR LAST DAY ON EARTH
APPRECIATING EACH OTHER
FOR ALL THAT IT IS WORTH
I LOVE YOU SWEETHEART
I HOPE YOU HAVE A NICE DAY
BECAUSE YOU ALSO MAKE ME FEEL
SPECIAL IN EVERY WAY
GOOD MORNING

124)
AS THE NIGHT PASSES

I SIT IN SILENCE
THINKING ABOUT YOU
A BEAUTIFUL WAY
TO MAKE THIS LOVE TRUE
MY SPIRIT WANTS TO CREEP
INTO YOUR BEDROOM
YOUR MIND, BODY, AND SOUL
I DESPERATELY WANT TO GROOM
IF I COULD MAKE A WISH
FOR JUST A LITTLE WHILE
IT WOULD WARM MY HEART
TO SEE YOU SMILE
DEEPER AND DEEPER
AS THE NIGHT FLOWS
VISIONS OF YOUR FACE
THE WAY THAT IT GLOWS
MELTING IN A DESIRE
THAT TAKES MY BREATH AWAY
NOW I'M IN A TRANCE
FLOATING INTO ANOTHER DAY
I JUST WANT YOU TO KNOW
THAT YOU MEAN A LOT TO ME
THE BEAUTIFUL PART OF MY LIFE
IS LOVING YOU SO SWEETLY

125)
HEAT AND PASSION

DEEP RICH SPICES OF
LOVES COMBINATION
A PURENESS SO DEVINE
GODS CREATION
ONE DROP OF TRUE PASSION
TWO DROPS OF HEAT
ONE DOZEN ROSES
TO MAKE THE MOMENT COMPLETE
CANDLE LIGHT AND DINNER
SWEET SMELLING OIL
CHAMPAGNE AND STRAWBERRIES
TO BRING THE ROOM TO A BROIL
THE HEAT BEGINS TO RISE
AS THE CREAM RISES TO THE TOP
MY DESIRE TO TASTE YOU
NEVER TO WASTE A SINGLE DROP
THE HEAT BEGINS TO MELT THE ROOM
NO WORDS COULD EVER EXPRESS
HOW YOU MADE MY HEART
YOUR PERMANENT ADDRESS

126)
THE DARKSIDE

ON FRIDAY 11/22/02

MY LIFE TOOK A DRAMATIC TURN
EVERYTHING THAT WAS GOING WELL
WAS ABOUT TO BURN
WITH A WIFE AND CHILDREN
A CHECK IN MY POCKET
GONE FOR THREE DAYS
HIGH AS A ROCKET
$600.00 LATER
THE GUILT SAT IN
I'VE CREATED SOMETHING TERRIBLE
A DANGEROUS AND AWFUL SIN
NOW I'M ON THE DARKSIDE
EVERYTHING I SEE I DREAD
EVERYBODY IS RUTHLESS
THE WALKING DEAD
I HAVE TO FIND MY WAY BACK
BEFORE IT'S TOO LATE
I'M FEELING SICK
WHAT'S INSIDE OF ME I HATE
CROSSED BETWEEN THE THOUGHT
OF BEING A VICTIM OF HOMICIDE
BUT THE TRUTH OF THE MATTER IS
WHAT I'M DOING IS SUICIDE
IN THE PROCESS I'VE CREATED
A RIPPLE EFFECT
MY FAMILY NEEDS ME

AND THE BILLS I NEGLECT
CAUGHT IN A WEB
I NEED TO BREAK FREE
SO I CAN SEEK SOME HELP
TO PRY THIS DEMON OUT OF ME
I STAND BEFORE YOU TODAY
IN NEED OF A HELPING HAND
FROM ANYONE WHO HAS THE PATIENCE
AND BELIEVE IN A REAL MAN
I KNOW I'M BETTER THAN THIS
I'VE SEEN IT BEFORE
IT'S UGLY AND SICKINING
I CAN'T STAND IT ANYMORE
A LIFE TIME OF BUILDING
IN THIRTY SECONDS IT CAN DISAPPEAR
I DON'T WANT TO SPEND MY LIFE
LOOKING OVER MY SHOULDER AND IN FEAR
WHAT YOU SEE BEFORE YOU TODAY
IS A TRUE MAN WHO SLIPPED AWAY
THE CONSEQUENCES OPENED THE DOOR
FOR THE DEMON TO LEAD THE WAY
I NEED TO FIND MY SHEPARD
TO WASH ME FREE
SO I CAN DO WHAT IS RIGHT
FOR ME AND FAMILY

127)
BEAUTIFUL AND DEEP

IT'S ONE O'CLOCK AM
SO DIFFICULT TO SLEEP
BECAUSE MY MIND IS THINKING
OF SOMEONE BEAUTIFUL AND DEEP
IT'S IN MY HEART TO SAY
IT'S YOU I'M THINKING OF
ANOTHER BEAUTIFUL GIFT
THAT CAME FROM ABOVE
I HOPE THAT YOU CAN BARE WITH ME
WHILE I WORK SOME THINGS OUT
IT'S YOU THAT I'M FEELING
IT'S YOU I WANT TO BE ABOUT
AN ELECTRIFYING FEELING
IS GENERATING MY SPIRIT
I CAN FEEL IT CALLING ME
IT'S SILENT, BUT I CAN HERE IT
VIBRATING MY MASCALINE STRUCTURE
A SPECIAL LOVE I REQUIRE
FROM SOMEONE BEAUTIFUL AND DEEP
LIKE YOU I DESIRE

128)
A BEAUTIFUL WOMAN

A BEAUTIFUL WOMAN
IS MORE THAN A PRETTY FACE
SHE HOLDS HER SELF RESPECT
AND HER POSTURE IS IN PLACE
SHE'S THE KIND OF WOMAN
WHO BELIEVE IN GOOD HEALTH
BLESSED WITH A SPIRIT
THAT BRINGS HER MUCH WEALTH
SHE REPRESENTS HERSELF
WITH THE WILL TO HOLD FAST
HER POSITIVE NATURE
DOESN'T LET HER DWELL ON THE PAST
SHE'S SOFT SPOKEN AND FASHIONED
IN THE MOST PRECIOUS WAY
IT BRINGS THE GIFT OF LIGHT
TO THE MOST DARKEST DAY
A BEAUTIFUL WOMAN
WITH SO MUCH AND MORE
A BEAUTIFUL WOMAN
I HOPE AND DREAM FOR

129)
WALK W/ME

WALK WITH ME TO A PLACE
THAT NO ONE HAS EVER BEEN BEFORE
WHERE THERE IS HAPPINESS
LOVE IS FOREVER AND MORE
WALK WITH ME TO A PLACE
WHERE DREAMS COME TRUE
LIFE IS EVERLASTING
THE ROSES ARE RED AND BLUE
WALK WITH ME TO A PLACE
WHERE A RIVER OF MILK FLOWS
TO A LIGHT SO BRIGHT
FROM A RAINBOW THAT GLOWS
WALK WITH ME TO A PLACE
WHERE YOUR HEART CAN BE FREE
AND THE ANGELS SING SONGS
OF LOVE TO YOU AND ME

130)
RED ALERT

WE'RE UP AGAINST A WAR
THE WORLD IS ABOUT TO BURN
GUNS, DRUGS AND GASES
ANOTHER PAGE IS ABOUT TO TURN
FROM VALLEY LOW TO VALLEY HIGH
NO PLACE TO RUN OR HIDE
BECAUSE THE EPIDEMIC IS SPREADING
TO ALL FOUR CORNERS NATIONWIDE
THE POLITICAL WORLD OF POWER
IS ALL A MONEY GAME
TERRITORIAL FACTORS
GIVE THE PICTURE A NEW FRAME
GRAVES ARE BEING ROBBED
FOR SCIENTIFIC REASONS
THE WHEATHER IS CHANGING SO
YOU CAN'T EVEN TELL THE SEASONS
BIOLOGICAL CREATURES
WITH THREE LEGS AND TWO HEADS
ARE THE RESULTS FROM EXPERIEMENTS
THAT GOD ONLY DREADS
IT'S A RED ALERT
FLAMES ARE RISING HIGH
YOU CAN SEE IT FOR MILES
FROM THE GLOW IN THE SKY

131)
LOVE

A DEEP INSPIRATION
WITH A DELICATE TOUCH
ITS PASSION IS TENDER
AND OFFERS MUCH
WHO CAN DEFINE
SUCH A POWERFUL THING
ONLY THOSE WHO CAN APPRECIATE
ALL THEY CAN BRING
AN UNCONDITIONAL LOVE
SHOULD NEVER BE BROKEN
THE ROOTS ARE PURE
WITH A VOICE TRULY SPOKEN
LOVE IS LIKE A FLOWER
WHEN IT BEGINS TO UNFOLD
A BEAUTIFUL ATTRACTION
WITH A SCENT THAT TAKES HOLD
SENSITIVE AND UNIQUE
WITH A MEANING SO TRUE
GIVE ALL THE REASONS WHY
I LOVE YOU

132)
PIMP STYLE

DON'T THINK THAT I'M HUNGRY
OR DYING OF THIRST
I'M A STRONG WILLED MAN
WHO BELIEVES IN GOD FIRST
SO ACCEPT ME FOR WHO I AM
NOT FOR WHAT I CAN PRODUCE
DON'T THINK FOR ONE MINUTE
THAT I'M EASY TO SEDUCE
WE CAN MAKE THIS WORK
IF YOU JUST COME CLEAN
CAUSE IF YOU FLIP THE SCRIPT
I CAN BE JUST AS MEAN
I DON'T HAVE A PROBLEM
WITH GETTING THINGS RIGHT
I DO HAVE A PROBLEM WITH
UGLY THINGS PRETENDING TO BE LIGHT
YOU CAN HAVE ALL OF ME
MY CARDS ARE ON THE TABLE
BUT DON'T PUT ON A FRONT
IF YOU KNOW YOU'RE NOT ABLE
I CAN GIVE YOU A SAMPLE
OR MAYBE A SMALL TASTE
BUT IF YOU'RE NOT SERIOUS
I'LL TAX YOU FOR THE WASTE
TEN PERCENT WILL GO
TO WHERE ALL RESPECT IS DUE
AND THE OTHER PERCENT WILL GO
TO SOMETHING BRAND NEW

133)
DON'T FIGHT THE FEELING

MY HEART IS HURTING DEEPLY
YOUR LOVE I TRULY MISS
THOSE BEAUTIFUL EYES
PRETTY SMILE, A TENDER KISS
DEEP INSIDE YOU MOVE ME
WITH A POWER I CAN'T RESIST
YOU'RE THE KEY TO MY HEART
TO LOVE YOU TRULY I INSIST
LETS DO AWAY WITH OLD THINGS
THAT BELONG IN THE PAST
BUILD SOMETHING STRONG
STEADY AND HOLD FAST
I CAN'T FIGHT THE FEELING
I LOVE YOU BOO
I CAN'T DENY MY HEART
SO TRUE, SO YOU

134)
BY MY SIDE

I DON'T WANT TO LOOK BACK
AND CALL YOUR NAME
I WANT TO LOOK BY MY SIDE
SEE US WALKING THE SAME
I NEVER WANT TO HAVE A REASON
TO THINK TWICE OR DOUBT
ANYTHING THAT WE'VE BECOME
OR EVEN BE ABOUT
I NEED TO FEEL
THAT TOGETHER WE CAN WIN
I NEED YOU BY MY SIDE
THROUGH THICK AND THIN
I WANT TO GIVE YOU LOVE
TRUST YOU WITH MY LIFE
HOPE THAT SOMEDAY SOON
YOU WOULD BECOME MY WIFE
I WANT TO DREAM OF YOU
EVEN WHEN I'M AWAKE
I WANT YOU TO BE
EVERY BREATH I TAKE

135)
MY LADY

WHEN I TAKE A DEEP BREATH
I FEEL THIS CHILL INSIDE OF ME
I SAY TO MYSELF
IS THAT MY LADY FEELING FREE
ALWAYS ON MY MIND
HER SPIRIT CONTINUES TO CREEP
SOMETIMES SHE CATHCES ME OFF GUARD
EVEN IN MY SLEEP
WITH AN OVER FLOWING FEELING
THAT MAKE ME WANT TO MELT
I STEP BACK AND SAY TO MYSELF
IS THAT MY LADY I FELT
IT'S SO TRULY AMAZING
HOW SHE IS EVERYWHERE I GO
SHE IS THE REASON FOR
MY SMILE, MY GLOW
OVER WHELMED WITH THIS FEELING
DEEP INSIDE OF ME
I SAY TO MYSELF ONCE AGAIN
IS THAT MY LADY FEELING FREE

136)
DESTINATION

MY HEART IS LIKE A MAP
OF RIVERS AND STREAMS
FLOWING IN ALL DIRECTIONS
WITH HOPES AND DREAMS
WITH A FIRM FOUNDATION
MY GOALS I HOPE TO ACHIEVE
THOUGHT IS THE CAUSE OF ALL THINGS
A PLAN I DO BELIEVE
MY GOAL IS TO BE SUCCESSFUL
PRODUCTIVE EVERYDAY
WITH A STRONG POSITIVE NATURE
THAT MAKE ME CREATIVE IN EVERY WAY
I WANT TO LIVE TRULY
LIKE I'VE NEVER LIVED BEFORE
I WANT A TASTE OF LIFE
THAT IS GOOD TO THE CORE
I CAN'T WASTE ANYMORE TIME
OR LET MY FIRE GO OUT
I HAVE TO DEFINE MY PURPOSE
OF WHAT I'M ALL ABOUT
WITH LOVE AND APPRECIATION
IN MY HEART I HOLD
THIS IS THE BASE OF MY LIFE
A STORY TO BE TOLD

137)
DON'T HOLD BACK

TELL ME WHAT YOU LIKE
YOUR DEEPEST DESIRE
I'LL CREATE A POTION
WITH A CREATIVE FIRE
TELL ME WHAT YOU FEEL
WHEN I LAY INSIDE OF YOU
LET ME WHISPER IN YOUR EAR
THINGS I WANT TO DO
LETS COME TOGETHER
TO MAKE IT ALL COMPLETE
LAY BACK IN THE MOISTURE
THAT CREATED ALL THIS HEAT
LETS DRINK SOME CHAMPAGNE
TAKE A SHOWER BY CANDLE LIGHT
DON'T HOLD BACK THE FEELING
CAUSE TONIGHT IS YOUR NIGHT
TELL ME WHAT YOU LIKE
MY FLAVOR TONIGHT
SWEET LOVELY LADY
MY STAR LIGHT

138)
DON'T FIGHT THE LOVE

LET YOUR LOVE POUR DOWN ON ME
AN OVER FLOWING STREAM
OF HEAT AND TRUE PASSION
RELEASING SO MUCH STEAM
LETS BOND A LOVE SO THICK
YOU CAN CUT IT WITH A KNIFE
A KIND OF LOVE THAT FREEZES
FOR LIFE
360 DEGREES
AROUND AND AROUND WE GO
A ROSE TO SYMBOLIZE MY LOVE
HOW STRONG WE WILL GROW
EXPRESSING YOUR TRUE FEELINGS
IN THE MOST DESIRABLE WAY
YOUR VOICE SPEAKS SOFTLY
WORDS OF LOVE YOU SAY
A MELTING CONTENTNESS OF LOVE
WARM IN HEART, LONGING TO KEEP
SO DEVINE, AND PRECIOUS
IT FLOWS IN YOUR SLEEP

139)
TONIGHT'S SPECIAL

IT'S LATE AT NIGHT
I'M ALL ALONE
I WOULD GIVE ANYTHING
TO HERE A SOFT TONE
MELTING WITH DESIRE
TO PLEASE YOU FIRST
THE THOUGHT OF MAKING LOVE
QUENCHES MY THIRST
I NEED YOU MY LOVE
TO MAKE THIS NIGHT COMPLETE
FULFILL MY DESIRE
WITH YOUR BODY HEAT
WITH RED ROSES AND CHAMPAGNE
DINNER BY CANDLE LIGHT
YOU'RE THE SPECIAL OF MY DESIRE
ON THE MENU TONIGHT

140)
O' LORD

O'LORD IN HEAVEN
CAST YOUR LIGHT ON ME
I CARRY MY CROSS
I DELIVER IT TO THEE
TO BARRY ALL OF MY BURDENS
ALL OF MY CONFLICTIONS
THE HOLY SPIRIT IS NOW
MY TOTAL ADDICTION
HUMBLE ME LORD
GRANT MY SOUL PEACE
THAT I MAY LIVE FOREVER
AND YOU I'LL NEVER RELEASE
ALLOW ME TO DIE O'LORD
SO THAT I MAY LIVE AGAIN
FOR THE LIFE THAT LIVES WITHIN ME
IS A LIFE WITHOUT SIN

141)
WORK THROUGH ME

LET THE PURPOSE OF YOUR PLAN
INCREASE WITHIN ME
MANIFEST YOUR THOUGHT
TO FULFILL YOUR PROPHECY
ALL THROUGH MY DAY
I WILL PRAISE YOU WITH LOVE
CAUSE EVERY GREAT GIFT
COMES FROM ABOVE
USE ME BY ALL MEANS
AS AN EXAMPLE OF YOUR WILL
SPEAK TO ME O'LORD
HOLD ME STILL
LET THE DELIVERENCE OF YOUR WORD
BE WISE AND BOLD
FOR THE SAKE OF SAVING ANOTHER
LET LIFE UNFOLD
SPEAK TO ME O'LORD
GRANT ME THE POWER
TO HELP ANOTHER SOUL
AT THIS VERY HOUR
LET THE LIGHT OF YOUR TEMPLE
WORK THROUGH ME
FOR THE SAKE OF SALAVATION
SETTING A SOUL FREE

142)
THANK YOU LORD

I'M SO GRATFUL
FOR THE PEACE TO SUSTAIN
THROUGH MANY TROUBLES
STILL LOVE I CONTAIN
WITH A ATTITUDE OF GRADITUDE
FOR SO MUCH MORE
MY LOVE INCREASES
LIKE NEVER BEFORE
YOUR FAVOR IS AMAZING
MIRACLES APPEAR
YOUR PRESCENCE I FEEL
WITHIN THE ATMOSPHERE
EACH AND EVERYDAY
THE MORE I BELIEVE
HOW MY FAITH
HAS ALWAYS BEEN THE KEY
FOR THE BLESSINGS I HAVE RECEIVED
YOU'VE ANSWERED ALL OF MY PRAYERS
AS I PATIENTLY AWAIT
FOR THE AUTHOR OF MY LIFE
TO DIRECT MY FATE
THANK YOU O'LORD
FOR THIS TIME WITH YOU
AS I WAIT FOR THE NEXT INSTRUCTION
OF WHAT I MUST DO

143)
SPIRITUAL STRENGTH

THE BEGINNING OF LIFE
IS TO HAVE SPIRITUAL STRENGTH
A SPIRIT THAT OVER RULES ALL
BEYOND THE MEASUREMENT OF LENGTH
IT'S THE ROOT THAT MAKE THE SOUL
THE BODY, THE MIND
MANIFESTED FROM THE LIKENESS
OF ITS OWN KIND
THE IMAGE WITHIN THIS SPIRIT
CAN ONLY BE SEEN
THROUGH A PURE AND RIGHTEOUS LIVING
BY KEEPING YOUR HEART AND MIND CLEAN
WITH A SINCERE HEART OF BELIEF
THIS SPIRITUAL STRENGTH WILL SUSTAIN
A FAITH OF TRUE PATIENCE
A WILL TO MAINTAIN
WHEN EVERYTHING ELSE MAY FALL
THIS STRENGTH WILL HOLD
TO A GREATER STRENGTH MORE POWERFUL
A STRENGTH MORE BOLD
A PRICELESS GIFT TO BEHOLD
THE BLESSING OF SPIRITUAL STRENGTH
A SPIRIT THAT RULES OVER ALL
BEYOND THE MEASUREMENT OF LENGTH

144)
OPEN HOUSE

I WISH YOU GUYS WOULD CHILL
I'M BUSY CAN'T YOU SEE
I CAN'T SPEND TONIGHT TRIPPING
AND RECITING POETRY
THE OLD MAN GOT THE HITS
READY TO TAKE THE SHOW
LETS GIVE HIM SOME RESPECT
LET THE OLD GEAZER FLOW
HIS POETRY IS VERY GOOD
FROM A PRO I'VE BEEN LISTENING
TO GIVE MY HONEST OPINION
THERE'S SOMETHING MISSING
POETRY HAS A RHYME
FROM THE BEGINNING TO THE END
IT'S THE POWER IN WORDS
IF YOU CAN COMPREHEND
DON'T TAKE IT PERSONAL
BECAUSE WE ARE ALL GROWN MEN
OR YOU WILL FIND YOURSELF IN SEG
WITHOUT A BUDDY OR A FRIEND
JUST KICKIN A LITTLE HUMOR
A LITTLE SOMETHING TO PASS THE TIME
CAUSE YOUR POETRY IS BUMPING
IT JUST NEEDS A BOTTOM LINE

145)
NOSY PEOPLE

HE SAY, SHE SAY
THAT'S ALL THEY TALK ABOUT
SOMETIMES STARTING FIRES
THEY CAN'T PUT OUT
DAY IN DAY OUT
WITH NOTHING BETTER TO DO
THEY SPEND ALL THEIR PRECIOUS TIME
FOCUSSING ON YOU
WITH FALSE INTENSIONS
THEY WILL LOOK INTO YOUR EYES
TRY TO SPEAK THE TRUTH
THROUGH A WINDOW OF LIES
IF YOU ARE A NOSY PERSON
THEN THIS MESSAGE IS FOR YOU
SEARCH DEEP DOWN INSIDE
FOR SOMETHING BETTER TO DO
WHAT YOU HAVE PUT OUT THERE
WILL EVENTUALLY COME BACK
THIS ALSO MAY BE THE REASON
WHY YOUR LIFE IS OFF TRACK

146)
TOUGH TIMES DON'T LAST

TOUGH TIMES DON'T LAST
BUT TOUGH PEOPLE DO
TIME HOLDS THE MEMORIES
OF THE PRESENT AND THE PAST
THE EVOLUTION OF LIFE
BRINGS THINGS THAT LAST
THROUGH TRIALS AND TRIBULATIONS
WE FIGHT TO SUCCEED
WE LEARN TO RESPECT AND APPRECIATE
WITHOUT SELFISHNESS OR GREED
OUR DIRECTION IS WHAT WE CHOOSE
TO SEEK OUR OWN DESTINY
MISTAKES ARE WELL LEARNED
OPEN MINDED WE WILL BE
WHAT WE VALUE IN OUR HEART
HOW STRONG WE TRULY BELIEVE
IS TO BE HONORED
FOR ALL THE THINGS THERE IS TO ACHIEVE
AT TIMES WE SEARCH FOR ANSWERS
FOR CERTAIN THINGS WE HOPE TO FIND
WITHOUT REALIZING IT'S ALREADY THERE
IN HEART AND IN MIND
AS WE LIVE TO ONLY SURVIVE
ONE DAY AT A TIME, DARKNESS TO LIGHT
WE PRAY AND HOPE WITH CONFIDENCE
FOR MORE STRENGTH TO FIGHT

147)
A BEAUTIFUL STAR

LOVE YOURSELF
ALL THAT YOU ARE
GOD MADE YOU TO BE
A BEAUTIFUL STAR
KEEP YOUR HEAD UP
REACH FOR THE SKY
ACCOMPLISH YOUR DREAMS
ENJOY YOUR HIGH
THERE MAYBE TIMES
WHEN YOU MAY FAIL
REMEMBER WINNERS DON'T QUIT
THEY JUST PREVAIL
BE CAREFUL OF THOSE
WHO TRY TO BRING YOU DOWN
THEY ARE THE ONES
WHO NEVER LEAVE THE GROUND
PROTECT YOURSELF WITH
A BOUNDARY, A SHIELD
BE THE BEST THAT YOU CAN BE
WITHIN YOUR FIELD
JUST KEEP STRIVING
TO REACH THE TOP
ALWAYS LOVE YOURSELF
AND DON'T EVER STOP
LET NOTHING OR ANYBODY
CHANGE WHAT YOU BELIEVE
JUST FOLLOW YOUR HEART
YOU WILL ACHIEVE

148)
PRAISE GOD

ONCE AGAIN MY LORD
YOU HAVE ANSWERED MY PRAYERS
I'VE ALLOWED YOU TO MANAGE
ALL OF MY AFFAIRS
HOW MUCH MORE
AM I WORTHY OF
I PRAISE YOUR FAVOR
HONOR YOUR LOVE
CONTINUE TO USE ME
AS A VESSEL BY WILL
USE ME TO DELIVER
LOVE AND FULFILL
YOUR HAND IS MIGHTY
AND REACHES FAR
THE LIGHT FROM THE EAST
THE BRIGHTEST STAR
I PRAISE YOU LORD
EVERY MINUTE OF THE DAY
CAUSE YOU ARE THE ANSWER
THE ONLY WAY

149)
O' FATHER IN HEAVEN

MY TEARS ARE FLOWING FASTER
THAN THEY CAN EVAPORATE
MY SOUL IS BEING DRAINED
I CAN NO LONGER PENETRATE
THE WORLD HAS BECOME A BURDEN
UPON MY HEART, MY HEAD
O'FATHER DO NOT LET ME FALL
TO BE A PART OF THE WALKING DEAD
IT IS YOUR REFUGE THAT I SEEK
YOUR PROTECTION I NEED
FUEL ME WITH THE HOLY SPIRIT
TO CULTIVATE THY SEED
DRY UP MY PUDDLES
WHERE MY TEARS BECAME A FLOOD
CONVICT ME WITH YOUR SPIRIT
WASH ME WITH YOUR BLOOD
O' FATHER IN HEAVEN
FOR I AM YOUR CHILD
EMBRACE ME WITH YOUR LOVE
DO NOT LET ME RUN WILD

150)
INNER PEACE

SOMETHING SOME MANY SEARCH FOR
VERY FEW FIND
A FEELING DEEP WITHIN SELF
A HUMBLE STATE OF MIND
THIS INNER PEACE
IS DEEP WITHIN THE CORE
ONCE YOU HAVE FOUND IT
YOU WILL EXPERIENCE A FEELING LIKE NEVER BEFORE
IT'S THE PEACE THAT OVER POWERS
CIRCUMSTANCES AND SITUATIONS
CARRIES YOU THROGH
TRIALS AND TRIBULATIONS
THERE ARE TIMES
WHEN WE MAY FAIL
INNER PEACE IS THE STRENGTH
TO OVERCOME AND PREVAIL
THE KINDNESS OF THIS PEACE
SHOWS LOVE TO MY SISTERS, MY BROTHERS
IT'S A SINCERE FEELING AVAILABLE
FOR ONE ANOTHER
IT SHEDS LIGHT ON DARKNESS
CHANGES WRONG TO RIGHT
IT BUILDS UP HOPE AND FAITH
AND A WILL TO FIGHT

151)
IT'S BEEN A VERY LONG WALK

IT'S BEEN A VERY LONG WALK
BEFORE I CAME TO THIS DAY
THROUGH TRIALS AND TRIBULATIONS
ONE OF THE SHEEP GONE ASTRAY
I FOUND MYSELF AT THE END OF THE ROAD
THEN I SUDDENLY STARTED TO CRY
AT THE POINT WHERE I WAS STANDING
IT DIVIDED INTO A Y
SO I RAISED MY HANDS AND FELL TO MY KNEES
TO PRAY FOR THE RIGHT DIRECTION
BUT I FIRST HAD TO CLEANSE MYSELF
WITH A HONEST CONFESSION
TO BE FORGIVEN OF ALL MY SINS
THROWING AWAY MY PRIDE
I'M IN THE MIDDLE OF TWO ROADS
ONE NARROW AND ONE WIDE
I OPENED MY EYES
AND RAISED TO MY FEET
AS A PICTURE CAME TO MY HEAD
THE ROAD TO THE RIGHT WAS FULL OF LIFE
AND ON THE LEFT WAS THE WALKING DEAD
I TOOK THE ULTIMATE STEP
UNDERSTANDING WHERE I BEEN BEFORE
I CHOSE THE ROAD TO LIFE
BECAUSE I CRAVE FOR SO MUCH MORE
AFRAID OF WHAT WAS IN STORE
A MIGHTY VOICE SAID TO ME
I'M USING YOUR LIFE
AS A TESTIMONY

152)
SILENT RAGE

AN ACTIVE FORCE
TO THIS VERY DAY
LOOKING TO DEVOUR
ANYTHING IN ITS WAY
A WALKING TIME BOMB
JUST WAITING TO EXPLODE
THE MOST DANGEROUS WEAPON
LOCK AND LOAD
IT COMES IN ALL FORMS
CAN BE IN ANY PLACE
SOMETIMES IT REPRESENTS
A SMILING FACE
WITH A COMBINATION OF TENTION
FRUSTRATION AND PAIN
IT HOLDS NO MERCY
AND NOTHING TO GAIN
A MENTAL BONDAGE
OF INVISIBLE VIOLENCE
A DESTRUCTIVE FORCE
THAT CREEPS IN SILENCE

153)
SATAN

YOU USE TO BE ONE OF GODS ANGELS
UNTIL YOU WERE FOUND IN VIOLATION
NOW YOU'RE FACING A PENALTY
OF A DIFFERENT REVELATION
I REFUSE TO GIVE YOU THE SATISFACTION
TO LIVE IN MY HEAD RENT FREE
I REFUSE TO GIVE YOU THE LEVERAGE
TO HAVE CONTROL OVER ME
I KNOW ABOUT YOUR PLAN
THE PIT AND THE LAKE OF FIRE
I KNOW THAT YOU ARE REAL
BUT I ALSO KNOW THAT YOU'RE A LIER
I'M NOT WORRIED ABOUT YOU'RE SCHEMES
OF ANY FASHION OR ANY FORM
CAUSE I'M PROTECTED BY THE BLOOD
THAT CARRIES ME THROUGH EVERY STORM
SO JUST ACCEPT THE FACT
THAT THIS SOUL YOU WILL NOT WIN
CAUSE I'VE BEEN CLEANSED BY THE BLOOD
THAT WASHES AWAY SIN

154)
YOUR COMFORT

A HOME OF COMFORT
IS ALL I SEEK
THE WORD OF TRUTH
O'LORD SPEAK
A FIRE THAT BURNS
THE WARMTH THAT I NEED
THE WORDS OF TRUTH
FOR FOOD TO FEED
COVER ME O'LORD
WITH YOUR BLANKET OF PROTECTION
YOUR" LOVE, YOUR MERCY
AND YOUR" AFFECTION
ALLOW ME O'LORD
TO REST IN YOUR PLACE
WHERE LOVE HONORS ALL
PEACE, LOVE, AND GRACE

155)
FULL SPEED AHEAD

NOTHING CAN BREAK MY STRIDE
I'M GOING FULL SPEED AHEAD
I'VE BEEN BLESSED WITH A NEW LIFE
THE OLD MAN IS DEAD
I WILL NOT WORRY ABOUT THE THINGS
THAT I CANNOT CONTROL
I'LL TURN IT OVER TO THE LORD
WHO IS ALWAYS NOURSHING MY SOUL
AGAINST THE SINS OF TEMPTATION
I FIGHT A MIGHTY POWER
WITH A SPIRIT THAT GROWS WITHIN ME
EVERY MINUTE AND EVERY HOUR
THERE'S NO TURNING BACK NOW
I'M HOOKED ON THE HOLY GHOST
I BREATH THE HOLY SPIRIT
AND I HAVE JESUS AS MY HOST
I FEEL MY SALVATION
ETERNAL LIFE I WILL SEE
BECAUSE GOD KNOWS MY HEART
IN JESUS I DO BELIEVE
IF I HAVE NOTHING
BUT WATER AND BREAD
I'M STILL GOING TO SEE THE GLORY
CAUSE I'M FULL SPEED AHEAD

156)
OPEN DESISRE

I'M THE MAKER AND MASTER
OF MY OWN DESTSINY
NOBODY BUT GOD
KNOWS WHAT'S GOOD FOR ME
LIFE IS FULL OF DREAMS
SO MANY BEAUTIFUL PLACES
WHERE THE SUN SHINES BRIGHT
ON COLORFUL FACES
SOMEWHERE IN THIS WORLD
THERE'S A LOVE JUST FOR ME
ONE THAT I HOPE
WILL LAST TILL ETERNITY
I WILL GIVE MY LIFE
FOR WHAT I FEEL INSIDE
TO ENJOY THE PLEASURE OF LOVE
SO MANY TIMES I'VE TRIED
ALTHOUGH I'LL NEVER GIVE UP
UNTIL THE END OF TIME
SOMEWHERE OUT THERE
THERE'S A LOVE THAT WILL SOON BE MINE

157)
CALL ME

WHEN YOU ARE LONLEY
AND NEED SOMETHING TO DO
I'LL BE YOUR FRIEND
A GENTLEMAN SO TRUE
LET ME DO THE WORRYING FOR YOU
RELIEVE YOU OF YOUR PAIN
BRING YOU BACK TO REALITY
SO MANY THINGS TO GAIN
WHEN YOUR HEART IS HURTING
OR BROKEN IN HALF
I'LL BE THE ONE TO HEAL YOU
WITH A HUG, AND A LAUGH
WHEN TIMES GET HARD
AND YOU DON'T UNDERSTAND WHY
YOU CAN CALL ON ME
I WILL ALSO CRY
ALWAYS REMEMBER THAT YOU
WILL NEVER HAVE TO BE ALONE
CAUSE MY FRIENDSHIP WITH YOU
IS LIKE THE TEXTURE OF STONE

158)
SOMEBODY TAKE ME

SO MUCH OF ME
IS MELTING AWAY
I HOPE TO FIND LOVE
BEFORE I EVAPORATE SOMEDAY
EVERYDAY AND EVERY NIGHT
IS FILLED WITH HOPES AND DREAMS
AN ENDLESS ROAD
IT ALWAYS SEEMS
WHY MUST I SUFFER
DOESN'T ANYONE LOVE ME?
FOR I'VE GIVEN MY HEART
AND ALL I CAN BE
MY JOY AND PLEASURES
ARE ALWAYS ON THE RUN
AN INTENSE DESIRE
THAT BURNS LIKE THE SUN
NOW I'M TIRED
READY TO SETTLE WITH LIFE
KICK BACK AND ENJOY
A TENDER AND BEAUTIFUL WIFE

159)
RUNNING OUT OF TIME

HOW FAR CAN I RUN
BEFORE MY LIFE IS DONE
I WILL GIVE MY ALL
TO BE CONNECTED AS ONE
DESPERATELY I TASTE A DESISRE
TO DEEPELY UNITE
WITH SOMEONE SPECIAL
ON THIS LONELY NIGHT
I CRY IN DEEP SILENCE
MY HEART IS FULL OF TEARS
FROM THE EMPTINESS INSIDE
I'VE BEEN CARRYING FOR YEARS
AS LONELINESS TAKES ITS TOLL
I'M GETTING SO WEAK
HANGING ON BY MY FAITH
TRUE PASSION I STILL SEEK
WITH ONE LAST BREATH
I HOPE TO ENHALE
A LOVE THAT IS WRITTEN
BETTER THAN A FAIRY TALE

160)
A SOUL WITHOUT A NAME

A PREMEDITATED THOUGHT IS SIMMERING IN MIND
SOMETHING IS ABOUT TO COLLASPE
THIRTY SECONDS OR LESS
FROM A POSSIBLE RELASPE
LIVING BEYOND MY MEANS
TO PLEASE THE WORLD AND EVERYTHING
MORE PRESSURE, MORE TENSION
THE MORE PAIN IT CONTINUES TO BRING
THE SPIRIT WITHIN ME IS DRAINED
WORKING SO HARD PLAYING CATCH UP
WHILE EVERYTHING ELSE IN LIFE
IS PASSING ME UP
SO AFRAID OF WHAT IS IN STORE FOR ME
MYSELF I MUST SAVE
A GRIP, SOME KIND OF HOLD
A FIRM FOUNDATION I CRAVE
AS TIME CONTINUES FORWARD
A DARK CLOUD HANGS OVER MY HEAD
AS I CRY OUT LOUDLY TO THE LORD
PLEASE SAVE ME FROM THE WALKING DEAD
I SEEK TO EMBRACE MY SALVATION
THE WRONG PICTURE IS IN THE FRAME
CAUSE THE LAST THING THAT I EVER WANT TO BE
IS A SOUL WITHOUT A NAME

161)
THE VALUE OF LOVE

THE VALUE OF LOVE
IS SINCERE AND NICE
AN UNCONDITIONAL EMBRACE
WITHOUT A PRICE
IT PROVIDES A COMFORT
WHERE THERE'S FEAR
SAYS THE RIGHT THINGS
TO DRY UP A TEAR
AN AUTOMATIC RESPONSE
TO HELP SOMEONE UP
AND WHEN YOU'RE THIRSTY IT SAYS
DRINK FROM MY CUP
AN UMBRELLA THAT WILL LAST
THROUGH ALL KINDS OF WEATHER
THE SECURITY OF KNOWING
WE WILL ALWAYS BE TOGETHER
A SPIRT THAT PLEASES
DESIRES AND NEEDS
THE BEST OF QUALITY TIME
IT ALWAYS FEEDS
A COMPASS FOR ONE
LOOKING FOR DIRECTION
A HEART FULL OF LOVE
CARE AND AFFECTION
A FEELING THAT UNDERSTANDS
THE PAIN ON ONES FACE
CAUSE THERE ONCE WAS A TIME
WHEN YOU STOOD IN THE SAME PLACE

IT'S BEING ABLE TO SEE EYE TO EYE
SHARING THE KEYS TO RELATE
FROM COMPROMISING TO UNDERSTANDING
THE PURPOSE TO COMMUNICATE
KNOWING WHEN ONE IS WEAK
THE OTHER SHOULD BE STRONG
WITHOUT KEEPING A RECORD
OF RIGHT OR WRONG
THE VALUE OF LOVE
CAN MEND A BROKEN HEART
IT COMES IN PEACE
AND NEVER FAR APART
IT'S LIKE THE FLOW OF THESE WORDS
WITH A CONSISTANT RHYME
THE VALUE OF LOVE
IS QUALITY TIME

162)
CAPTURED BY THE LIGHT

I FIND MYSELF CAPTURED
EVERY NIGHT
BY THE MOST BEAUTIFUL
RAY OF LIGHT
QUICKLY I PRAY
WITHOUT BLINKING A EYE
AS IT GRACEFULLY FLOATS
ACROSS THE SKY
AT THE SAME TIME
IN THE SAME PLACE
I FIND MYSELF CAPTURED
BY THIS GLOW OF GRACE
EACH AND EVERY NIGHT
I FEEL A DEEP INCREASE
THAT GRANTS MY SOUL
WITH THE LIGHT OF PEACE
WITH EAGERNESS I WAIT
I KNOW IT WILL BE SOON
I FIND MYSELF CAPTURED
BY THE LIGHT OF THE MOON

163)
THE VICTIM

A LONG TIME AGO
I WAS IN THE WRONG PLACE
AT THE WRONG TIME
WHEN EVERYONES ISSUES
SUDDENLY BECAME MINE
MY KINDNESS WAS TOTALLY TAKEN
TO BE SOMEONE VERY WEAK
MY LIFE BECAME A BIG HOLE
WITH A CONSTANT LEAK
BEING USED AND ABUSED
IN THE MOST INHUMANE WAY
SOME OF THESE THINGS I CAN'T SPEAK ON
TO THIS VERY DAY
TAUNTED BY THE VISIONS
OF FACING SO MANY FEARS
MY LIFE WAS UNBARABLY PAINFUL
WITH SO MANY TEARS
AFRAID OF WHAT WAS IN STORE FOR ME
TRYING TO MAKE THE RIGHT CHOICE
CRYING OUT FOR HELP
NO ONE HEARD THE SOUND OF A BROKEN VOICE
LIKE A RIVER OVER FLOWING
THE SINS BECAME A FLOOD
THAT REVEALED A PICTURE OF MYSELF
LYING IN MY OWN BLOOD

164)
A NEW BEGINNING

I'VE WAITED FOR THIS MOMENT
WITH FAMILY I LONG TO BE
THE GATES HAVE FINALLY OPENED
TO SET THIS MAN FREE
RIDING DOWN THE HIGHWAY
IN WHAT I BELIEVE IS A CAR
HURRY UP AWAY FROM THIS PLACE
TAKE ME FAR
WHEN I GET TO WHERE I'M GOING
I WANT TO TAKE A WALK
KICK IT WITH ALL OF YOU
LAUGH AND TALK
THE MOMENT WILL BE INSPIRING
TEARS OF HAPPINESS WILL POUR
THEN WE'LL GATHER LATER
CELEBRATE SOME MORE
BUT BEORE I GO ANY FURTHER
LITTLE FACES I NEED TO SEE
OF THOSE WHO HAVE BEEN CRYING
AND TRULY MISSING ME
THEN I WILL BEGIN
MY DUTY AS A MAN
HOLDING DOWN MY RESPONSIBILITIES
WITH A POSITIVE PLAN
SEE YOU LATER

165)
TODAY

TODAY IS TODAY
SO LIVE IT ALL THE WAY OUT
FORGET ABOUT YESTERDAY
OR YOU WILL THROW TODAY IN DOUBT
TODAY YOU CAN BE THANKFUL
CAUSE TOMORROW IS NO GUARANTEE
THE BREATH OF LIFE
IS LIKE A BUD ON A TREE
TODAY IS A DAY
THAT SHOULD BE TRULY GLORYIFIED
BE CONTENT WITH ALL YOU HAVE
TRY TO BE SATSIFIED
TODAY IS A BLESSING
TO BE GRATEFULL FOR
CAUSE WHEN TOMORROW COMES
TODAY WILL BE NO MORE
TODAY IS A MIRACLE
JUST TAKE A LOOK AROUND
IF YOU LISTEN CLOSELY
THERE'S A VARIETY OF SOUND
TODAY IS ALL YOURS
YOU CAN MAKE IT GOOD OR BAD
YOU HAVE A CHOICE
TO BE HAPPY OR SAD
TODAY IS THE DAY
TO EXPRESS YOUR MIND
MANIFEST YOUR THOUGHTS
FOR A PURPOSE TO FIND
TODAY WILL SOON BE A VAPOR
OF HOPES AN DREAMS
SO LIVE IT TO THE FULLEST
AND FOR EVERYTHING IT MEANS

166)
TO UNDERSTAND ME

IS TO LOVE ME FOR WHO I AM
NOT FOR WHO YOU THINK I SHOULD BE
SOMETIMES I MAY BE BLIND
THEN PLEASE HELP ME SEE
AS MY INTENTIONS UNFOLD
MY OPIONIONS MAY AT TIMES VARY
BLESSED IS MY SOUL
LOVE I WILL ALWAYS CARRY
THERE MAY BE A TIME
WHERE MY HEART IS IN PAIN
YOUR LOVE COULD BE THE STRENGTH
I NEED TO REGAIN
SOMETIMES I MAY REACH
FOR THINGS I CANNOT SEE
AND MY BELIEF MAY GO BEYOND
YOUR UNDERSTANDING FOR ME
THAT IS WHY FAITH IS THE SUBSTANCE
TO HOPE AND TO DREAMS
THEREFORE I AIM TO LIVE FOR ALL THAT IT'S WORTH
NOT FOR WHAT IT SEEMS

167)
BRIDGES

REMEMBER THE BRIDGE
THAT YOU ALWAYS COULD CROSS
AND NOW ALL OF A SUDDEN
IT SEEMS A TOTAL LOSS
HAVE YOU EVER GOT TO A PLACE
AND THEN DECIDED TO TURN
CAUSE A MEMORY IN YOUR MIND
SUDDENDLY STARTED TO BURN
WHAT ABOUT THAT BRIDGE
THAT'S FALLING ALL APART
FROM LIES, BETRAYAL
AND NOW A BROKEN HEART
REMEMBER THAT SPECIAL BRIDGE
YOU ALWAYS USE TO MEET
HAS IT EVER CROSSED YOUR MIND
WHY IT'S NOW BENEATH YOUR FEET
REMEMBER THE OPPORTUNITY YOU HAD
TO HARVEST A GLORIOUS CROP
BUT BECAUSE OF YOUR SELFISHNESS
YOU COULDN'T REACH THE TOP
AND WHAT ABOUT THAT BRIDGE
THAT IS NOW A PILE OF DUST
FROM THE LACK OF LOYALTY
HONESTY AND TRUST

168)
WE LIVE AND LEARN

EVERY WHERE WE GO
HIS CREATION IS RIGHT BEFORE OUR EYES
WE HAVE TO BE CAREFULL
THE WORLD IS FULL OF LIES
HIS WORD MAKES THE LAW
THAT JUDGEMENT TO THIS VERY DAY
THERE IS NO ESCAPE
JESUS IS THE ONLY WAY
BY THE POWER OF FAITH
HOW MUCH YOU BELIEVE
IS THE MEASUREMENT OF LOVE
THE VALUE OF DEED
WISDOM IS IN THE HEART OF THOSE
WHO ARE WILLING TO LEARN
BUT THE EVIL SNARES OF TEMPTATION
WILL CAUSE YOU TO BURN
HE'S A BLESSING IN DISQUISE
MERCIFUL IN HEART
IF YOU DON'T KNOW HIM NOW
IT WOULDN'T HURT TO START

169)
FOREVER ALIVE

I SIT IN SILENCE
TO WRITE WHAT I FEEL
I BYPASS THE FAIRY TALES
TO EXPRESS WHAT IS REAL
I HAVE A STRONG HEART
A LOT ON MY MIND
I WRITE ABOUT THE THINGS
THAT I HOPE TO FIND
IT'S MY WAY OF TRAVELING
A SPIRITUAL RIDE
TO RELEASE A PRESSURE
THAT BURNS INSIDE
IT'S MY WAY OF FREEDOM
A SOURCE TO GET AWAY
TO REACH ALL REALITY
A SPECIAL WAY TO PRAY
I'LL NEVER FORGET
THE POWER THAT EXISTS
THE CREATOR OF AUTHORITY
I WILL NEVER RESIST
I'M BLESSED TO BE ALIVE
WITH SO MUCH MORE TO GAIN
MY NAME IS WRITTEN IN HEAVEN
AS MY SOUL WILL ALWAYS REMAIN

170)
RUNNING DRY

YOU'RE SO CLOSE
BUT YET SO FAR AWAY
MY HEART IS CRYING
FOR LOVE IN A SPECIAL WAY
SHARE WITH ME
EVERYTHING THAT YOU FEEL
AND I'LL GIVE YOU IN RETURN
A LOVE THAT IS REAL
SIGNED SEALED AND DELIVERED
WITH MUCH TO APPRECIATE
I HAVE IN MY HEART
A LOVE TO DEDICATE
WAITING O SO PATIENTLY
FOR MY ONLY SOUL MATE
TO BUILD A BRIDGE OF BEAUTY
A LOVE TO CREATE
IT'S IN MY HEART TO BELIEVE
THAT SOMEDAY SHE WILL APPEAR
THE DREAM OF MY LIFE
WILL MAKE IT FOREVER SO CLEAR
THIRSTY FOR LOVE
MY HEART IS BLEEDING DRY
I FOLD MY HANDS AND PRAY
FOR AN ANGEL TO WIPE MY EYES
FOR ALL THAT IT'S WORTH
I'LL GIVE MY BEST TO SATISFY
WITHOUT A SECOND THOUGHT
I WILL ALWAYS TRY

171)
ONE DAY

ONE DAY I'LL BE FREE
TO SHARE MY INSPIRATION
A DEDICATION OF LOYALTY
A FAITHFUL DEVOTION
THERE WILL BE A TIME
WHEN I'LL REACH MY DESTINY
CAUSE THE KING OF SALVATION
HAS A CROWN JUST FOR ME
I'VE MADE A CONFESSION
FOR ALL OF MY WRONG
I'VE CHANGED MY LIFE
TO BE POSITIVE AND STRONG
I HAVE A DREAM
THAT I STRONGLY BELIEVE
MY LIFE IS NEW
MY PAIN IS FREE
NOW I CAN LIVE
IN THE QUALITY OF LIGHT
TO SEE THINGS CLEARLY
AS MY TALENT TAKES FLIGHT
WITH EVERYTHING TO HONOR
IN THIS LIFE I BELIEVE
THAT WITHOUT HOPE
I'LL NEVER BE FREE

172)
I TRUST YOU WITH MY LIFE

MY LIFE I GIVE TO YOU
WITH DEDICATION AND DEVOTION
I PROMISE TO CARRESS YOUR TEARS
YOUR" EVERY EMOTION
I CAN'T HELP THE WAY I FEEL
MY LOVE HAS TAKEN FLIGHT
FROM THE LOVE THAT YOU SHARE WITH ME
DAY AND NIGHT
MY FAITH, MY TRUST, MY EVERYTHING
I OFFER YOU MY LIFE
ALL THE THINGS THAT ARE BEAUTIFUL
FOR A SWEET LOVING WIFE
IN THE PALM OF YOUR HAND
YOU HOLD THE KEY TO MY HEART
TOGETHER WE WILL MEND A BOND
THAT WILL NEVER PART
MIND, BODY AND SOUL
MY WORLD REVOLVES AROUND YOU
EVERYTHING I FEEL
IS IN THE SPECIAL THINGS YOU DO

173)
GENTLY

GENTLY I WANT TO STROKE YOU
IN THE MOST AFFECTIONATE WAY
LEAVING YOU WITH A FEELING
THAT NO WORDS COULD EVER SAY
GIVING INTO A PASSION
SO HARD TO RESIST
THAT THE HEAT BEGINS TO MELT
MY MIND BEGINS TO TWIST
GENTLY I WANT TO STROKE YOU
UNTIL SWEAT BEGINS TO DRIP
YOUR VOICE SINGS SOFTLY
AS I FINALLY REACH THE TIP
COVERING YOU WITH MANY KISSES
CAUSING A NATURAL HIGH
A FOUNDATION OF LOVE SO DEEP
IT WILL NEVER RUN DRY
GENTLY I WANT TO STROKE YOU
WITH THE LOVE OF A FRIEND
A KIND OF LOVE THAT WILL LAST FOREVER
FROM BEGINNING TO END

174)
YOU CAN DO IT

LET'S TALK ABOUT TRUTH
THE POWER OF THE CONSCIOUS OF THE MIND
IF YOU SEEK WITHIN YOURSELF
THERE'S NO TELLING WHAT YOU MAY FIND
EVERYONE HAS DREAMS
SECRETS AND FANTASIES
SOME HAVE HIDDEN TALENTS
AND OTHERS DIFFERENT DESTINIES
IT'S A MATTER OF CHOICE
WHICH EVER WAY YOU CHOOSE
IT'S THE GAME OF LIFE
SOME WIN, SOME LOOSE
YOU HAVE THE ABILITY
TO BE WHAT IS IN YOUR HEART
LET NOTHING CHANGE YOUR MIND
DON'T FALL APART
UNDERSTAND THAT FAILING
ISN'T ALWAYS A BAD THING
EXPERIENCE IS THE BEST TEACHER
KNOWDLEDGE AND WISDOM IT CAN BRING
THE SPIRIT IS THE KEY
THE LIMIT IS THE SKY
YOU DON'T MISS THE WATER
UNTIL THE WELL RUNS DRY

175)
FOREVER IN YOU

IF I COULD BE WITH YOU
I WOULD ONLY KEEP IT REAL
MY INFACTUATION WITH YOU
IS SHARING ALL I FEEL
I FIND YOU VERY ATTRACTIVE
IN THE QUIET WAY YOU TALK
AND THE POWER OF YOUR AUTHORITY
WITH THAT SMOOTH SEXY WALK
YOUR INTELLECTUAL MIND
MYSTIFYING AND SO MESMORIZING
YOUR" INDEPENDENCE
SO RELYING, SO SATISFYING
I WILL SHARE WITH YOU A ROMANCE
OF CAPTIVATION
I WILL STIMULATE YOUR HEART
WITH A BRIDGE OF COMMUNICATION
I GIVE MY FULL HONOR
AS I SET THE PACE
CREATING A DRIVE WITHIN YOU
THAT WILL LEAVE US TOGETHER AND LOST
WITHOUT A TRACE

176)
THE MOTHERS OF THE WORLD

MOTHERS ARE VERY SPECIAL PEOPLE
THERE HEARTS ARE DEEP AND SINCERE
LOVE FOR FAMILY
ALWAYS NEAR
IT'S IN THERE DEEPEST CONSIDERATION
TO HAVE PRIDE IN WHAT THEY DO
THE MEASUREMENT OF THERE DEEDS
HOLDS RESPECT FOR ME AND YOU
STRONG AND GIFTED
WITH THE POWER OF RESPONSIBILITY
AND DEPEND ON THE MOST HIGH
FOR THE GREATEST SECURITY
MOTHERS ARE BEAUTIFUL PEOPLE
WHO PUT THERE LIVES ON THE LINE
I'LL ALWAYS BE PROUD TO SAY
THAT MOTHER IS MINE
MOTHERS ARE THE PEOPLE
WHO GIVE THE STRENGTH TO BARE
THERE THE KIND OF PEOPLE
WHO WILL ALWAYS BE THERE
SO BLESSED ARE THE MOTHERS
WHOS WILL IS TO PRAY
FOR WE ALL LOVE DEARLY
HAPPY MOTHERS DAY

177)
QUICK SAND

I FOUND MYSELF FALLING
DEEPER THAN I'VE EVER FELL BEFORE
AN INTENSIFYING LOVE
THAT MAKES ME WANT HER EVEN MORE
DEEPER AND DEEPER I'M FALLING
TO WHAT SEEMS AN ENDLESS PIT
ON MY WAY DOWN
I SEE CANDLES LIT
I SEE HER BEAUTIFUL FACE
SO WARM AND TENDER
SHE'S ALL THE PRECIOUS THINGS
I'LL ALWAYS REMEMBER
DEEPER AND DEEPER I'M FALLING
AS MY HEART BEGINGS TO VIBRATE
TO GIVE HER ALL OF MY HEART
WHATEVER IT MAY TAKE
SHE MESMORIZES MY SOUL
SHE HAS CAPTIVATED MY HEART
YOU'RE THE WOMAN I FELL IN LOVE WITH
FROM THE VERY START

178)
I'M ADDICTED TO YOU

MY ADDICTION FOR YOU
I CAN'T SHAKE
IT'S SOMETHING NEW
I CAN'T SEEM TO BREAK
MANY NIGHTS I TOSS AND TURN
SO HARD TO REST
IT'S NO SECRET
I'VE TAKEN ON THE BEST
HOT FLASHES, COLD FLASHES
AN UNCONTROLABLE SWEAT
DREAMS OF YOU SO DEEP
IT MAKES ME WET
YOUR LOVE IS SO GOOD
WITH ITS DEVESTATING BITE
MAKES ME SURRENDER
WITHOUT A FIGHT
A HIGH SO BEAUTIFUL
THAT MAKES ME DROP TO MY KNEES
TO SATISFY YOUR DESIRE
I'LL DO WHATEVER TO PLEASE
THE MOST ULTIMATE HIGH
THAT I'VE EVER FELT
BEING IN LOVE WITH YOU
JUST MAKES ME MELT

179)
ARE YOU TRULY GRATETFUL

DO YOU REALLY KNOW HOW GRATETFUL IT IS
TO BE HERE TODAY
DID YOU SHOW YOUR APPRECIATION
DID YOU EVEN PRAY
ARE YOU ASKING FOR THINGS BEFORE
GIVING THANKS FOR WHAT YOU'VE ALREADY GOT
JUST THE FACT THAT YOU HAVE LIFE
SAYS THAT YOU'VE BEEN BLESSED WITH A LOT
DID YOU PRAY FOR SOMEONE TODAY
WHO IS WORSE OFF THAN YOU
DO YOU REALLY KNOW HOW BLESSED YOU ARE
IS THE LOVE INSIDE OF YOU TRUE
CAN YOU GO THROUGH THIS ONE DAY
WITHOUT PASSING JUDGEMENT ON ANOTHER
RATIONALIZING DIFFERENCES OR FAULT FINDING
INSTEAD OF PRAYING FOR A BROTHER
ARE YOU TRULY GRATEFUL
FOR WHAT YOU HAVE TODAY
IF YOU HAVEN'T YET
NOW IS THE TIME TO PRAY

180)
MY BLACK QUEEN

MY BLACK QUEEN
SO BEAUTIFUL AND WISE
WITH A SMILE THAT GLOWS
AND PRETTY BROWN EYES
A BURNING PASSION OF DESIRE
CRIES OUT FOR YOUR TOUCH
TO HEAR THE SOFT TONE OF YOUR VOICE
SAY I LOVE YOU SO MUCH
IF I COULD MAKE MYSELF VANISH
AND THEN REAPPEAR
I WOULD ROLL DOWN YOUR FACE
IN THE FORM OF A TEAR
WITH THE MOST ARTICULAR STYLE
OF PLEASING AND SATISFACTION
YOU'RE THE HIGHLIGHT OF MY LIFE
MY EVERY ATTRACTION
WHAT WE HAVE TOGETHER
IS SO DELICATE AND DEVINE
I LOVE MY BLACK QUEEN
SO BEAUTIFUL AND FINE

181)
IN MY ROOM

AS I SIT IN MY ROOM
WITH SHADES OF BLUE
I START VISUALIZING
BEAUTIFUL THINGS ABOUT YOU
THE DEEPNESS OF YOUR SOFT TONE
THE LIFE BEHIND YOUR EYES
THE ENCHANTING PERSONALITY
OF A WOMAN SO WISE
YEARING TO HAVE
LOVE AT ITS FULLEST CAPACITY
MOISTURE ABSORBS IN OUR PORES
OF SOLVING EACH OTHERS CURIOSITY
TO TAKE FULL ADVANTAGE OF THIS MOMENT
TO LAY MY SOUL AND MY HEAD TO REST
AGAINST THE TEXTURE OF LOVE
YOUR SOFT BEAUTIFULL BREAST
AS I SIT IN MY ROOM
WITH SHADES OF BLUE
I START VISUALIZING
BEAUTIFUL THINGS ABOUT YOU

182)
YOU CAN'T STOP WHAT'S GOING TO HAPPEN

THE STORY OF MY LIFE WAS WRITTEN
FOR THE SOLE PURPOSE TO TRANSPIRE
A GIFT FROM GOD
ETERNAL LIFE AND AN EVERLASTING FIRE
ALL THAT I MAY ENCOUNTER
FOR PURPOSE OR REASON
GIVES A FACT TO THE MATTER
THAT EVERYTHING HAS A SEASON
IT'S NOT BY ACCIDENT
THAT I WAS A PART OF GODS PLAN
TO FULFILL A DREAM
OF A QUALIFIED MAN
NOT BY MY OWN WILL
THAT I HAVE THE POWER TO STAND
IT'S BEYOND MY CONTROL
I'M CALLED BY DEMAND
THEREFORE I'LL EMBRACE LIFE
WITH EVERYTHING AND MORE
BECAUSE ALL THAT EXISTS NOW
HAS EXISTED BEFORE

183)
SISTERS

YESTERDAY HOLDS THE MEMORIES
OF WHAT SOCIETY HAS DONE TO ME
THE CRUELTY OF SLAVERY
AND A BROKEN FAMILY
TODAY IS A NEW TIME AND AGE
FOR THE LIGHT IN ME IS NOW FREE
TO BE PROSPEROUS AND STRONG
FOR THE UNITY OF FAMILY
SEEKING MY HIGHER ABILITIES
GOD HAS GIVEN ME A CHANCE
TO CREATE WHAT IS IN MY MIND
AND THE FIELD TO ADVANCE
I'M THE WOMAN OF YESTERDAY
WHO HOLDS THE SPIRIT TO BELIEVE
THAT ALL THE DOORS OF POSSIBILITIES
ARE NOW OPEN FOR ME.

184)
BACK HOME

THER'S A LITTLE PLACE
WHERE I WAS BORN AND RAISED
WHERE THE PEOPLE WERE GENTLE
AND THE LORD THEY PRAISED
A PLACE OF FAMOUS HISTORY
THE OLD SANTA FE TRAIL
HOME OF HARRY S. TRUMAN
WHOSE NAME IS WRITTEN IN BRAILLE
WITHIN THIS LITTLE PLACE
ALWAYS SOMETHING TO DO
AND THE HIGHEST LEVELS OF EDUCATION
ARE TAUGHT IN SCHOOL
THE HOUSES ARE OLD FASHIONED
THE QUALITY GREW FROM A SEED
THE LAND WAS CULTIVATED
FOR FOOD AND NEED
THE PLACE WHERE I WAS RAISED
UNDER OLD JUDGE AND JURY
THE PLACE WHERE I WAS RAISED
INDEPENDENCE MISSOURI

185)
LOVING YOU

NOTHING COULD EVER WEIGH MORE
THAN THE LOVE I HAVE FOR YOU
A MELTING AND INTENSE DESIRE
OF A PASSION SO SINCERELY TRUE
DEDICATED AND DEVOTED
TO YOUR MENTAL AND PHTSICAL ATTRACTION
YOU'RE THE CURE FOR MY HEART
MY EVERY SATISFACTION
LOVING YOU IS LOVING LIFE
A SPECIAL QUALITY SO RARE
SO SWEET, SO HONEST
SO BEAUTIFUL YOUR" CARE
A MYSTIFYING HEART OF GOLD
THIS I TRULY MISS
THE TENDERNESS OF YOUR TOUCH
A SOFT WARM KISS
I PRAY FOR YOU TONIGHT
NOW I MUST CLOSE
AS I PICTURE YOUR BEAUTIFUL FACE
IN THE MIDDLE OF A ROSE

186)
ALREADY SAVED

WE ARE ALL ONE BODY
DEEP WITHIN THE SPIRIT
CAUSE IT'S THE WORK OF THE LORD
WE ARE ALOUD TO FEAR IT
BY THE STROKE OF EVERY MINUTE
GROWING STRONGER WITH HIS MIGHT
LOOK OUT SATAN
CAUSE YOU'RE IN FOR A FIGHT
EVEN WHEN WE ARE SLEEPING
HE IS CREEPING THROUGH THE NIGHT
THE LORD IS OUR PROTECTOR
OUR SAVIOUR AND OUR LIGHT
I KNOW ABOUT YOU SATAN
FROM THE STREETS TO THE PRESS
YOU DON'T SCARE US
CAUSE WE'VE ALREADY BEEN BLESSED
SO BACK OFF SATAN
THIS IS WHERE THE RIGHTEOUS LIES
HAVEN'T YOU HEARD YET
THAT IT'S THE EVIL THAT DIES

187)
IN CHANGE COMES GROWTH

WE LIVE BY THE SEASONS
IN GROWTH COMES CHANGE
TO ACCEPT THE PURITIES OF BLESSINGS
THAT ARE WELL IN RANGE
ON THIS SPECIAL OCCASION
WE SHARE LAUGHS AND SMILES
SENDING OUT GIFTS
THAT TRAVEL FOR MILES
TO SHARE THIS MOMENT WITH YOU
IS A VISION SEEN SO CLEAR
THE FEELING OF TRUE WARMTH
OF A HEART SO NEAR
THE NEW YEAR HAS COME
LOVE AND HAPPINESS WE SHARE
SPECIAL THOUGHTS OF CONCERN
OF TENDER LOVING CARE
TO YOU I SEND MY BLESSINGS
OF VALUE IN A SPECIAL WAY
HOPING THAT EVERYTHING GOES WELL
THROUGH THE HOLIDAY

188)
LIFE WITH THE SPIRIT

ADAPTING TO CHANGE
TAKING OWNERSHIP
SURRENDERING
LISTENING TO THE SPIRIT
GIVING BACK
HOPE
FAITH
UNDERSTANDING
WISDOW
KNOWLEDGE
RESPECT

THE ONE ABOVE ALL OF THESE IS LOVE, WITHOUT IT THERE IS NO LIFE! LOVE IS THE KEY TO EVERYTHING, BEGINNING WITH GOD FIRST, YOURSELF, AND THEN FOR OTHERS, A DEVELOPING SPIRITUAL NATURE THAT SHINES LIGHT ON DARKNESS AND IS RECOGNIZED THROUGH ITS WALK, TALK, ACTIONS, AND DEEDS.
WALKING WITH THE SIGNS OF LOVE IS BEING ABLE TO ENDURE A GREAT DEAL OF SUFFERING FROM THE WORLD BECAUSE THE CLOSER YOU BECOME TO GOD THE MORE PERSECUTION YOU FACE. TRIALS AND TRIBULATIONS MAY BECOME BOLDERS OF GREAT WEIGHT, BUT GOD WILL NEVER PUT ON YOU MORE THAN YOU CAN HANDLE AND NO WEAPON FORMED AGAINST YOU SHALL PROSPER THEREFORE, BE STILL, AND HOLD FAST. FALL IN FAVOR WITH GOD TO RECEIVE THE PURPOSE AND THE BLESSING THAT IS CHOSEN FOR YOU!
ALTHOUGH IT IS NOT GOING TO EASY, IT CAN BE DONE BECAUSE YOUR TESTIMONY ALONE IS LIVING PROOF, SO DON'T QUIT BEFORE THE MIRACLE HAPPENS.

189)
LIGHT

WHEN WE HEAR THE WORD "LIGHT" WE USUALLY THINK OF DAYLIGHT OR ELECTRIC LIGHT, AND YET THE SAME WORD IS USED IN RELATION TO KNOWLEDGE. FOR EXAMPLE, A PERSON WHO IS ENLIGHTENED IS VERY KNOWLEDGEABLE. TO HAVE SEEN THE LIGHT SIGNIFIES AN END TO IGNORANCE, AND WE HAVE ALL HEARD THE PHRASE, LET THERE BE LIGHT. WE MIGHT ALL GIVE MORE MEANING TO THE WORD LIGHT IN OUR INDIVIDUAL WORLD.

COULD ONE OF OUR GOALS BE TO SEARCH FOR MORE LIGHT AND UNDERSTANDING IN OUR LIVES, AND THE LIVES OF THOSE AROUND US?

THIS COULD BE OUR CONTRIBUTION TO MORE PEACE, HARMONY, AND HAPPINESS IN OUR EVERYDAY EXISTENCE.

TRY ADDING MORE LIGHT TO YOUR LIFE AND YOU'LL FIND YOURSELF MUCH MORE PRONE TO GIVE THANKS THAN COMPLAINTS.

190)
THE PATH

*SO MANY OF US ARE SEEKING A PATHWAY TO FOLLOW.
THERE ARE NUMEROUS INDIVIDUALS, EACH WITH
TEACHINGS THAT THEY BELIEVE WILL BENEFIT
ANOTHER, AND EACH FEELING IN THEIR PARTICULAR
APPROACH FAR OUTSHINES OTHERS.
BUT EVEN KING SOLOMON WITH ALL OF HIS WISDOM
COULD NOT HAVE SHOWN US THE WAY. IT IS ONLY AFTER
TRUE ENLIGHTENMENT THAT WE REALIZE THAT EACH
PERSON HAS HIS OWN PERSONAL ROUTE DOWN THE
ROAD OF LIFE.
PATHWAYS, LIKE PEOPLE ARE UNIQUE, AND EACH HAS
A CHARACTER OF ITS OWN. INSTEAD OF LOOKING FOR
SOMEONE ELSE TO FOLLOW, SEARCH FOR YOUR OWN
SPECIAL PATHWAY, FOR EACH INDIVIDUAL SHOULD
LEARN TO KNOW THAT YOU ARE YOUR OWN, AND YOU
ARE THE MAKER AND MASTER OF YOUR OWN DESTINY.*

191)
WISDOM

KNOWLEDGE IS SOMETHING WE ALL HAVE TO PASS ON TO OTHERS. HOWEVER, THE FACT THAT A PERSON IS KNOWLEDGEABLE IN A NUMBER OF AREAS DOES NOT MEAN HE IS NECESSARILY ENDOWED WITH WISDOM. A VERY WISE INDIVIDUAL IS ONE WHO HAS A GREAT DEAL OF INSIGHT. WISDOM SEES BEYOND THE OBVIOUS TO THE HIDDEN WORKING OF THE MIND. ONE BECOMES CONSCIOUS OF CAUSES RATHER THAN EFFECTS OF SUCH CAUSES. LOOK TO THE RARE PERSON OF WISDOM AND YOU WILL BE IMPRESSED BY THE FACT THAT THE WISE ARE NOT GIVEN INTO QUICK JUDGEMENT BUT OFFER GREAT UNDERSTANDING TO THE MOTIVATION OF OTHERS. WISDOM BROUGHT TO ANY SITUATION HAS THE CAPACITY TO BRING ORDER TO WHERE THERE IS CHAOS, KNOWLEDGE TO WHERE THERE IS IGNORANCE. IN YOUR SEARCH FOR KNOWLEDGE, TRY TO MAKE WISDOM A CONSTANT COMPANION. TO SECURE KNOWLEDGE, IS TO ALSO KNOW THE TRUTH, BECAUSE THE TRUTH WITHIN THE KNOWLEDGE OF WISDOM GIVES BIRTH TO UNDERSTANDING.

192)
FAITH

THE MOST SUCCESSFUL PEOPLE IN THE WORLD ARE THOSE WITH A DEEP ABIDING FAITH IN THEMSELVES. A PERSON WHO BACKS UP HIS DREAMS WITH FAITH WILL NOT BE SHAKEN NO MATTER HOW DIFFICULT THE ROAD TOWARD ACCOMPLISHMENT. WITH FAITH WE CAN SAY, I DON'T KNOW HOW I'M GOING TO FULFILL THIS DREAM, I ONLY KNOW I AM. VERY FEW PEOPLE RECOGNIZE THE VAST POTENTIAL THEY HAVE WITHIN THEMSELVES AND ARE NOT LIKELY TO DISCOVER IT WITH A MENTALITY THAT SAYS, I DO NOT KNOW HOW. HAVE THE FAITH TO TAKE THE STEPS NECESSARY TO LEAD YOU TO YOUR GOAL AND YOU WILL FIND HIDDEN TALENTS YOU NEVER EVEN KNEW EXISTED WITHIN. HAVE FAITH AND YOU CAN INDEED ACCOMPLISH IN LIFE THAT WHICH WILL GIVE YOU GREAT PRIDE AND JOY.

193)
EVIL

*IT'S A SPIRIT THAT LURKS IN THE SHAWDOWS, IT IS
A DISTRUCTIVE SPIRIT THAT HAS THE PATIENCE A
HUNDRED TIMES BEYOND OUR IMAGINATION, IT IS A
SPIRIT THAT IS AN EXPERT OF TRICKERY AND ATTACKS
AT TIMES ON A UNCONSCIOUS AND CONSCIOUS MIND.
IT IS A POWERFUL FORCE THAT NEEDS TO FEED ON IT'S
ON ENERGY, IT NEEDS A SOUL TO WORK, AND THEN IT
TAKES THAT SOUL AND USES IT TO RECRUIT OTHERS. IT'S
A PHYCOLOGICAL AND MANIPULATING POISON THAT
SPREADS LIKE A DISEASE AND HAS NO MERCY ON IT'S
VICTIMS AND DOES NOT DISCRIMINATE. EVERY RACE
COLOR AND CREED IS IN DANGER OF THIS WICKED FORCE,
IT TEARS DOWN FAMILIES, MARRIAGES, FRIENDSHIPS,
GOALS, ACHIEVEMENTS AND SELF ESTEEM ATTACKING
EVERY ANGLE TOWARDS ANY MOTIVE ONE MAY HAVE FOR
RISING IN A GODLY NATURE AND WILL GO TO WHATEVER
MEANS NECESSARY TO GET ITS SATISFACTION. ITS MAIN
DEFINITION IS TO KILL! AT TIMES WE MAY EXERCISE AN
ACT OF BEHAVIOR THAT MAY QUESTION OUR MOTIVES
AND INTENTIONS CAN BE AT TIMES CONFUSING AND
MISLEADING TO OTHERS BECAUSE OF A PRIOR PATTERN
OF LIFE STYLE OR BEHAVIOR, BUT THAT DOESN'T MEAN
THAT THE INDIVIDUAL IS NOT TRYING TO LOOK FOR A
WAY OUT. SOME THINGS ARE NOT EASILY DEALT WITH AS
OTHERS ALL THOUGH MANY SOLUTIONS MAY COME TO
MIND THE WICKED HAS A WAY OF MAKING THINGS LOOK
OKAY WHEN IT REALLY ISN'T. DEEP WITHIN OURSELVES
WE ARE EXPERIENCING A SPIRITUAL WARFARE WHERE THE*

HIGHER SELF IS IN A SERIOUS BATTLE WITH THE LOWER SELF AND THE REALITY OF THIS MATTER SHOULD NOT BE IGNORED. THE ONLY WAY TO BEAT THIS EVIL FORCE IS TO SEEK A MUCH GREATER POWER THAN IT, (GOD)!!!!! THE ONE AND ONLY WAY BECAUSE THIS THING IS BIGGER THAN ANY OF US CAN EVER COMPREHEND AND DO NOT GET TO COMFORTABLE WITH DOING THINGS ON YOUR OWN CAUSE JUST WHEN YOU THINK YOU GOT IT THAT'S WHEN THE TRIALS AND TRIBULATIONS COME INTO PLAY AND FLESHLY TEMPTATIONS BECOME A THREAT TO YOUR OWN SOUL AND EVERYTHING THAT YOU THINK COULDN'T OR WOULDN'T HAPPEN BEGINS TO HAPPEN AND THE HARSH PART ABOUT IT ALL IS THAT IT IS USUALLY OUT OF OUR CONTROL BECAUSE OF THE CONSEQUENCES WE GO THROUGH AFTER THE CHOICE HAS BEEN MADE BECAUSE THOUGHT IS THE CAUSE OF ALL THINGS FIRST AND THE PREPERATION ON THAT THOUGHT IS IN THE PROCESS INSTANTLY.

TO BE AWARE, IS TO BE ALIVE

194)
LOVE THE BIRTH

IN ORDER TO BE ABLE TO LOVE IN ANY FORM OR FASHION YOU HAVE TO KNOW LOVE AND THE CHARACTERISTICS THAT COME WITH IT. TO KNOW YOURSELF IS TO KNOW LOVE BECAUSE YOU WERE MADE OF THE LIKENESS, THE IMAGE OF THE ONLY CREATOR OF LOVE. TO WALK IN LOVE IS TO ALSO UNDERSTAND THAT THE WORLD WILL HATE YOU AND YOUR PLAN TO MEET YOUR DEVINE PURPOSE, BECAUSE THE LAW OF LOVE IS ABOVE ANY AND EVERYTHING THAT THE WORLD HAS TO OFFER.
THINK ABOUT THIS:
HAVE YOU EVER TOLD SOMEONE YOU LOVE THEM JUST TO PACIFY A MOMENT FOR SELF BENEFIT? OR JUST FOR THE SIMPLE REASON TO BUY YOURSELF SOME TIME BECAUSE YOU NEVER WAS FEELING IT ANYWAY. BUT A TRUE LOVE WILL ALWAYS STAY IN TOUCH WITH LOVING CHARACTERISTICS.

195)
REVELATION

SITTING BACK AND REMINISING
ON THE OLD SCHOOL JAMS
THE PARTIES, THE LADIES
THE MONSTER SLAMS
WHAT HAPPENED TO THE LOVE
IT'S FADING AWAY
SO MUCH HAS CHANGED
SINCE YESTERDAY
THE WORLD IS FULL OF EVIL
WITH TRICKS AND GAMES
MANY FACES COME AND GO
WITH THOUSANDS OF NICK NAMES
THERE USE TO BE A TIME
WHEN LOVE WAS FREE
IN THIS DAY AND AGE
EVERYTHING HAS A FEE
FROM CONVERSATION TO WATER
EVEN AIR HAS A PRICE
THE JUDGEMENT BY LAW
MAKES YOU HUSTLE FOR A SLICE
THE CHILDREN ARE TRYING HARD
TO STAY HEALTHY AND STRONG
WHILE THE SYSTEM ACCUSES THEM
OF SO MUCH WRONG
THOSE THAT FAUGHT FOR OUR COUNTRY
FOR A MEDAL OR FOR A NAME
WENT DOWN IN HISTORY
FOR A PICTURE WITHOUT A FRAME

HOSPITALS, CHURCHES AND INSTITUTIONS
ARE ALL MONEY MAKING SCHEMES
THEY MANIPULATE A LOT OF THOUGHTS
WRECK A LOT OF DREAMS
THE HOMELESS AND HUNGRY
CRY FOR BREAD OR MILK
WHILE THE RICH AND FAMOUS
EAT STEAK AND WEAR SILK
THESE ARE THE THINGS
THAT'S BEEN GOING ON FOR YEARS
THERE'S NO BIG SECRET
ABOUT THE MULTITUDE OF TEARS
FAMILIES ARE FALLING APART
FROM LACK OF COMMUNICATION
MISERY BECOMES THE COMPANY
OF TENSION AND FRUSTRATION
WHAT HAPPENED TO PRIVACY
DOES ANY ONE KNOW
CAUSE NOW THEY HAVE SCOPES
THAT CAN TELL WHEN YOU COME
AND WHERE YOU GO
SO MANY OF US ARE QUICK
TO FIND FAULT IN ANOTHER
WHAT HAPPENED TO YOUR LIGHT?
MY SISTER, MY BROTHER
BABIES ARE HAVING BABIES
MANY HEARTS ARE BROKEN
SOME ARE SO AFRAID

OF BEING TRULY OUT SPOKEN
AND WHATEVER HAPPENED
TO THAT SO CALLED FRIEND
BECAUSE OF JELOUSY AND ENVY
EVEN THAT HAS COME TO A END
MARRIAGES ARE NOT AS COMMON
LIKE THEY USE TO BE
THE LOVE IS FADDING
CAN'T YOU SEE
I GUESS THIS IS THE END
THE FINAL CHAPTER
BUT ONE THING THAT IS FOR SURE
IT WILL BE MORE PLEASANT
IN THE WORLD HERE AFTER
I PRAY FOR ALL OF YOU
ANYTHING ELSE OF ME WOULD BE UNFAIR
I HOPE TO SEE YOU IN HEAVEN
CAUSE I WILL BE THERE

196)
FAMILY

It's a beautiful thing
To have such unity
When one is blind
The other can see
With love and concern
Family shouldn't fail
They should have a bond that states
We will prevail
Rain' sleet, snow or shine
Trials and tribulations
Is a true combination of
Understanding and communication
That makes a family strong
Shows for who they are
The strength of this love
Carries them far
Even in the moments of sadness
And feeling so far apart
You can still feel the love
Cause it comes from the heart
A family of this strength
Should always cherish
Because life is too short
It will soon perish

197)
THE CHOSEN ONE

AS I CLOSE MY EYES
I FELL INTO THE MOST DEEPEST SLEEP
I FOUND MYSELF IN A PASTURE
WITH THOUSANDS OF SHEEP
I LOOKED AROUND FOR A SHEPARD
FOR MILES I COULD NOT SEE
THOUSANDS OF SHEEP ALONE
WHO IS WATCHING OVER THEE?
THE STRANGEST THING CAME OVER ME
AS IF I'VE BEEN HERE BEFORE
THE CLOSER I GOT TO THE SHEEP
I BEGAN TO FEEL IT EVEN MORE
SUDDENLY ACROSS THE SKY
I SEEN MY PAST
AND ALL THE SHEEP HAD FACES
OF THOSE I SEEN LAST
THEN I BEGAN TO REALIZE
AS A LIGHT STOOD OVER ME
THAT I WAS THE CHOSEN SHEPARD
TO WHATCH OVER THEE
MY TEARS BEGAN TO FLOW
AS I BOWED TO HONOR THEE
FOR GRANTING ME THE GREATEST GIFT
A LIFE OF ETERNITY

198)
RESPECT ME

IT DOESN'T MATTER WHO I AM
I STILL DESERVE RESPECT
I'M A PERSON JUST LIKE YOU
NOT A WANT TO BE RE-JECT
DON'T TAKE MY KINDNESS
FOR SOMETHING TO BE WEAK
I'M BLESSED WITH A VISION
THE TRUTH I SPEAK
IF YOU CAN'T SAY ANYTHING NICE
DON'T SAY ANYTHING AT ALL
CAUSE THE CURSE YOU BRING ON ME
MAY CAUSE YOURSELF TO FALL
I HAVE A LOT OF LOVE
AND SOMETIMES I CAN BE WRONG
MY TRIALS AND TRIBULATIONS
HAS MADE ME VERY STRONG
SO IT REALLY DOESN'T MATTER
WHAT YOU THINK ABOUT ME
FOR THE LIGHT OF RIGHTEOUSNESS
WILL RISE ABOVE THEE

199)
WATCH OVER ME

O'LORD JESUS
PLEASE WATCH OVER ME
AS I LIE DOWN TO REST
I PRAY TO THEE
COVER ME WITH
YOUR PRECIOUS GLOW
FOR WHEN I RISE
YOUR LIGHT WILL SHOW
THANKYOU FOR THE STRENGTH
A NEW VIEW TO SEE
EACH AND EVERY SIGN
OF YOUR LOVE FOR ME
I SEEK OF YOUR UNDERSTANDING
FOR A WAY TO GO
TO DO WHAT IS RIGHT
ONLY YOU WOULD KNOW
O'LORD JESUS
PLEASE WATCH OVER ME
AS I LIE DOWN TO REST
I PRAY TO THEE

200)
WHAT I SEE

IF YOU COULD ONLY SEE
THROUGH THE CURTAINS OF MY EYES
A TRACK RECORD OF PROMISES
BROKEN HEARTS AND LIES
ROADS OF DISATERS
DETOURS I'VE TURNED
SOME BRIDGES CROSSED
SOME WERE BURNED
ROLLER COASTER RIDES
GOING UP AND DOWN
TRYING TO MAKE A LIVING
FROM TOWN TO TOWN
ALL THE SMILES AND LAUGHTER
TURNED INTO SADNESS AND PAIN
BROUGHT AN INSTANT SHOWER
OF TEARS THAT RAIN
ONCE THE STROM IS OVER
THE TRUTH BECOMES BRIGHT
BECAUSE WHATEVER IS IN THE DARK
WILL SOON COME TO LIGHT

201)
HOME BOUND

A NEW WAY OF LIFE
BETTER THEN BEFORE
A GARDEN OF FRUIT
AND SO MUCH MORE
GOLDEN GATES
FACES THAT SHINE
CROWNS AND DIAMONDS
CUT SO FINE
A HOUSE ON THE HILL
A RIVER THAT FLOWS
WITH SO MANY SPIRITS
SO MANY GLOWS
PARADISE BEHOLDS
A HOME TO PRAISE
WHERE HUMBLENESS AND PEACE
FOREVER LASTING DAYS
HOLY AND BEHOLD
IN HEAVEN I MUST BE
CAUSE IN ORDER TO SEE THIS BEAUTY
YOU HAVE TO BE FREE

202)
LIKE A DOVE

LIKE A DOVE YOU DESCEND
LANDING GENTLY ON ME
WARNING ME OF ALL THE THINGS
THAT ARE ABOUT TO BE
I TAKE SAFELY UNDER THY WINGS
YOUR PROTECTION I LONG FOR
AS YOU WHISPER TO ME
TO FEAR NO MORE
FOR I WILL GO AHEAD OF YOU
CLEAR THY PATH
WHO SO EVER INTERFERES
WILL FEEL THY WRATH
SO WALK IN PEACE MY SON
I'M THE LIGHT BY DAY
STAY STRONG IN THY FAITH
REMEMBER NOT TO SWAY
LIKE A DOVE YOU LANDED ON ME
I PRAISE YOUR FAVOR
LIKE A DOVE YOU LANDED ON ME
THANK YOU MY SAVIOUR

203)
WORKSHOP

TODAY I WILL PULL MYSELF
INTO YOUR WORKSHOP
FOR THE HIGHEST MAINTENACE
TO BE THE CREAM OF THE CROP
SPECIAL ADJUSTMENTS
IS WHAT I NEED
A FINE TUNING PROCESS
TO CULTIVATE THY SEED
FUEL ME UP O' LORD
WITH THE POWER OF YOUR WORD
SO THAT WHEN I SPEEK
I WILL TURLY BE HEARD
BREATHE THROUGH ME
THE BREATH OF LIFE
SO THAT I CAN STAND TRIALS
TRIBULATIONS AND STRIFE
FILTER MY SOUL O" LORD
MY BODY AND MY MIND
SO THAT ALL WILL BE ABLE
MY PURPOSE I SHALL FIND

204)
BEHIND ENEMY LINES

I TRUST YOU MY LORD
THAT NO HARM WILL FALL UPON ME
SHOW ME THE MIGHT
OF YOUR LOVE SO GRACIOUSLY
MY LIFE IS IN YOUR HANDS
I NEED YOUR UNDERSTANDING
I'VE SURRENDERED MY ALL
TO DO WHAT IS DEMANDING
EQUIP ME O" LORD
WITH THE ARTILLARY OF DEFENSE
LET YOUR WORDS BE MY POWER
AND BUILD AROUND ME A FENCE
LET MY ENEMIES BE SNARED
BY THEIR OWN PLOTS AGAINST ME
I LOOK UP TO YOU O" LORD
DEPEND ON TOTALLY
THE POWER OF YOUR WORDS
MY HEART CONTINUES TO HOLD
BEHIND ENEMY LINES
OF A WORLD SO COLD

205)
AS THE SEED UNFOLDS

AS THE SEED BEGINS TO UNFOLD
ITS ROOTS START TO SPREAD
THE WORD IS THE FERTILIZER
IT NEEDS TO BE FEAD
SUDDENLY HIGHER ABILITIES
BEGIN TO TAKE PLACE
IT SHOWS BY YOUR WALK, TALK,
AND THE GLOW ON YOUR FACE
DOORS BEGIN TO OPEN
IN WAYS YOU CAN'T IMAGINE
LIFE BECOMES A CLEAR FOCUS
OF GOOD THINGS WORTH HAVEN
THE EXPRESSION OF LOVE FLOURISHES
BY YOUR ACTIONS AND DEEDS
AND OUT OF THE RESULTS
IS THAT IT PLANTS MORE SEEDS
AS THE SEED UNFOLDS
A NEW LIFE BEGINS TO TAKE PLACE
THE VALUES IN WHICH IT BEHOLDS
IS THE EVIDENCE OF GODS GRACE

206)
THE ANGELS

I WAS ONCE TOLD BY AN ANGEL
THAT IT'S MY TURN TO ANSWER MY CALLING
TO REACH OUT AND TOUCH THE SOULS
OF THOSE WHO ARE LOST AND FALLING
A LIGHT HAS FALLEN UPON ME
TO TOUCH MY SISTERS AND BROTHERS
SO THEY CAN BE USED TO BE VESSELS TO REACH OUT
AND TOUCH OTHERS
I WAS TOLD BY AN ANGEL
THAT MY WORK HAS JUST BEGUN
BECAUSE THE LIFE HERE AFTER
THERE'S MORE WORK TO BE DONE
THE WORD HAS BECOME MY LIFE
HAS GIVEN ME A VISION TO SEE
THAT AS LONG AS I AM RIGHTEOUS
MY BLESSINGS WILL FALL BEFORE ME
I WAS TOLD BY AN ANGEL
TO PROCLAIM THE VICTORY
TO FULFILL THE PROPHECY
OF A KING IN THE MINISTRY

207)
04/05/61

A VERY SPECIAL DAY
LIFE HAS TURNED ANOTHER PAGE
I'M TRULY THANKFUL
TO FLIP A NEW AGE
ONLY TO LIVE A LIFE
I DON'T EVEN FEEL I DESERVE
BUT SINCE I'VE BEEN FAVORED
MY LORD I WILL SERVE
USE ME BY ALL MEANS
I'M AT YOUR COMPLETE DISPOSAL
AN APPLICATION TO FULFILL
TO DO ACCORDINGLY TO YOUR" WILL
EVERY MINUTE OF THE DAY
I PROMISE TO BE PATIENT
HOLD FAST AND NOT STRAY
YOU ADDED ANOTHER CHAPTER TO MY LIFE
BLESSINGS CONTINUE TO OVERFLOW
INSIDE AND OUT
YOU CONTINUE TO GLOW

208)
I SHALL NOT WORRY

I SHALL NOT WORRY
ABOUT WHAT TOMORROW MAY BRING
I HAVE YOU O'LORD
THAT'S EVERYTHING
I SHALL NOT WORRY
ABOUT THOSE WHO DO ME WRONG
YOU ARE MY PROTECTOR
THAT KEEPS ME STRONG
I SHALL NOT WORRY
ABOUT FOOD TO EAT
YOU ARE THE PROVIDER
OF MY BREAD AND MEAT
I SHALL NOT WORRY
ABOUT MONEY OR BILLS
YOU'RE MY PERSCRIPTION
WITH PLENTY OF REFILLS
I SHALL NOT WORRY
ABOUT GETTING TO AND FRO
CAUSE YOU WILL TAKE ME THERE
AND BRING ME BACK WHEN IT'S TIME TO GO

209)
TIME" WHAT IS TIME?

THE SPACE BETWEEN LIGHT AND DARK
FROM A FLASH OF LIGHTENING
TO THE SMALLEST SPARK
THE ESSENCE OF THE SPIRIT
THAT FORMED THE EARTH
OR THE SPACE BETWEEN CONCIEVING
OR GIVING BIRTH
THE SPACE BETWEEN
WHAT IS SLOW OR FAST
LIFE BEFORE DEATH
THE HISTORY OF YOUR PAST
THE EVIDENCE BETWEEN BEING ABLE TO LEARN AND
TEACH
THE DIFFERENCE BETWEEN THINGS
CLOSE AND OUT OF REACH
THE ENERGY OF WHAT IS
WEAK OR STRONG
OR THE FACTS THAT LIE
BETWEEN RIGHT AND WRONG
TIME IS THE SCIENCE
A MEASUREMENT OF DISTANCE
TIME IS THE CREATOR
OF EVERYTHING IN EXISTENCE
TIME DOESN'T CHANGE OR PASS AWAY
TIME IS LIVING
JUST FOR TODAY

210)
A WOMAN OF GOD

IS A WOMAN OF NOBLE CHARACTER
A MIRACLE OF CREATION
THE QUEEN OF THE LAW
WITH A DEEP APPRECIATION
HER INTELLECTUAL SPIRIT
GIVES HER A SPECIAL GLOW
HER WORDS ARE SOFT SPOKEN
WITH A GENTLE FLOW
WITH A DEEP UNIQUE STYLE
SHE HOLDS AN ATTRACTION
A COMBINATION OF HUMBLENESS
LOVE AND TRUE SATISFACTION
SHE HAS THE VISION TO FORSEE
CERTAIN SYMBOLS AND SIGNS
SHE KNOWS THE DIFFERENCE BETWEEEN
GOOD AND BAD DESIGNS
WITH A CREATIVE PURPOSE
A STRONG WILL TO PRAY
HER FAITH DEPENDS ON GOD
EACH AND EVERY DAY

211)
SACRAFICES

SOME ARE HARD TO GIVE UP
SOME ARE HARD TO QUIT
SOME ARE WRONG
SOME ARE LEGIT
THE SACRAFICES YOU MAKE
CAN ADD YEARS TO YOUR LIFE
SOME SACRAFICES CAN BRING
MORE DRAMA, MORE STRIFE
THE SACRAFICES YOU MAKE
COULD MEAN SUCCESS
ON THE OTHER HAND IT MAY MEAN
THAT YOU'VE SETTLED FOR LESS
A SACRAFICE COULD MEAN
GIVING UP YOURSELF
IT COULD ALSO MEAN
BUILDING UP YOUR HEALTH
WHATEVER SACRAFICES YOU MAKE
BE CAUTIOUS AND BE SURE
BECAUSE THE END RESULTS ARE
THE CONSEQUENCES YOU'LL ENDURE

212)
ARE YOU LISTENING

DO YOU REALLY HEAR
WHEN GOD SPEAKS TO YOU
DO YOU BELIEVE IN YOUR HEART
THAT HIS WORD IS TRUE
WHAT IF I TOLD YOU
A MIRACLE HAPPENED TODAY
WOULD YOU TAKE HOLD
OR JUST WALK AWAY
SUPPOSE I WAS TO TELL YOU
THAT THE WORD WILL SET YOU FREE
EVERYTHING THAT IS HAPPENING
WAS PREDESTINED TO BE
WOULD YOU THEN LISTEN
TO HIS HOLY VOICE
OR WOULD YOU NEGLECT THE BLESSING
OF HAVING A CHOICE
WHAT IF I WAS TO TELL YOU
THAT THE SAME VOICE TALKS TO ME
THEN WOULD YOU SEE THE REFLECTION
OF HOW WE ARE SUPPOSE TO BE

213)
BLESSINGS

Blessings can come
At any time or any place
Can turn a frown
Into a smiling face
Blessings can come
In many different ways
Some are short
And some last for days
Blessings are not always
In receiving, but in giving
This makes the value of life
So much worth living
Blessings can also
At times disappear
From the lack of being thankful
Or the lost of someone dear
Blessings are the gifts
From the creator above
The thoughts of the one
Who has true" Love"

214)
A SHED OF LIGHT

SOMETHING AS SMALL AS A TEAR
CAN MEAN SO MUCH
A SAD FACE COULD NEED
JUST A SIMPLE TOUCH
EVERYTHING WAS CREATED
TO RECEIVE AND RELEASE
ONLY TO WIN THE PROSPERITY
OF SALVATION AND PEACE
A MOMENT OF THANKSGIVING
TO BREAK BREAD
A MOMENT OF ANOITMENT
TO BE SPRIITUALY FEAD
AS THE SUN HIDES BEHIND THE CLOUDS
WATING FOR A SUDDEN BREAK
I PRAY TO THE LORD
MY SOUL TO TAKE
I HOLD MY PROMISE
TO DO WHAT IS RIGHT
AS I WAIT SO PATIENTLY
FOR A SHED OF LIGHT

215)
THE POWER OF PRAYER

JUST WHEN YOU'VE COME TO FEEL
THAT EVERY THING IS UNFAIR
JUST CALL ON GOD
THERES POWER IN PRAYER
WHEN YOU BEGIN TO FEEL WEAK
NO-ONE ELES IS THERE
JUST CALL ON GOD
THERES POWER IN PRAYER
WHEN YOUR HEART IS HURTING
FOR LOVING CARE
JUST CALL ON GOD
THERES POWER IN PRAYER
IF SUDDENLY YOU FEEL
THE LOAD IS TOO MUCH TO BARE
JUST CALL ON GOD
THERES POWER IN PRAYER
THE MIRACLE IS ALWAYS WORKING
TO BE ALIVE IS TO BE AWARE
JUST BELIEVE IN GOD
THERES POWER IN PRAYER

216)
TESTIMONIES

TESTIMONIES ARE TRUE LIFE STORIES
PREDESTINED FOR A REASON
FOR EVERYTHING HAS A PURPOSE
ALSO A SEASON
A DELIVERING MESSAGE
TO SAVE OR SHED LIGHT
TAKING ALL THAT'S WRONG
AND CONVERTING IT INTO RIGHT
IT'S A GIFT ONLY GIVEN
TO JUST A CHOSEN FEW
SOME ARE OLD
SOME ARE NEW
IT'S THE EVIDENCE OF THE TRUTH
FROM ALL YOU'VE BEEN THROUGH
A REFLECTION OF CHARCTER
OF ME, OF YOU
A TESTIMONY COULD MEAN
OVERCOMING STRIFE
A TESTIMONY IS SAYING
TODAY I HAVE LIFE

217)
THE FRONT LINE

I FIGHT FOR MY LIFE
EACH AND EVERY DAY
THE DEVIL IS OUT TO CRUSH ME
IN THE MOST DISTRUCTIVE WAY
HE WANTS TO TAKE MY FAMILY
HE WANTS TO TAKE MY JOB
HE WANTS ME TO SERVE THE WORLD
BECAUSE IT'S GOD HE WANTS TO ROB
I HAVE TO STAY FOCUSSED
ON WHAT I CAN'T SEE
PUT ON MY FULL ARMOUR
FOR THE SAKE OF SAVING ME
WITH THE WORD AS MY SWORD
SALVATION AS MY LIGHT
I'M FULLY EQUIPED
AND PREPARED TO FIGHT
A SOLDIER TO BEHOLD
SO PRECIOUS AND SO DEVINE
AS I FIGHT FOR MY LIFE
ON THE FRONT LINE

218)
ENOUGH IS ENOUGH

SIGNS AND SYMBOLS
ARE FOR THE CONSCIOUS MIND
SOLUTIONS TO ANSWERS
WE SO SEEK TO FIND
HAVE YOU EVER SAID TO YOURSELF
O' IT'S NOTHING AT ALL
ONLY TO FIND THAT SOMETHING LATER
CAUSED YOU TO FALL
THERE'S NO STRANGE HAPPENINGS
THE MESSAGES THAT ARE SENT
THEY'RE THE SOLUTIONS TO OUR PROBLEMS
THAT WE CAN PREVENT
BECAUSE WE IGNORE THE SIGNS
THAT SAY ENOUGH IS ENOUGH
IS THE REASON WHY OUR LIVES
SOMETIMES GET TOUGH

219)
FROM 1-10

HER WALK IS SO SEXY
HER TALK IS SO SMOOTH
I CAN TELL SHE HAS A POTION
TO HEAL AND SOOTH
WITH FINE BEAUTIFUL HAIR
PRETTY SMILE, PRETTY EYES
I CAN TELL THAT SHE IS UNIQUE
AND SO VERY WISE
A LIGHT GLAZE OF GLOSS
SHINES ON HER LIPS
THE ENERGY OF HER LIFE
OUTLINES THE CURVES OF HER HIPS
TEMPTING AND IRRESISTABLE
SHES KNOWS WHAT SHES GOT
FAR FROM BEING CONCEDED
JUST BLESSED WITH A LOT
TO KNOW THIS WOMAN
SO BEAUTIFUL, SO TENDER
IS TO KNOW A TRUE ANGLE
A BLESSING TO REMEMBER
A WOMAN OF CONFIDENCE
THAT I MAY NEVER SEE AGAIN
SHE WILL ALWAYS BE ON MY MIND
AS A PERFECT 10

220)
WHAT DOES IT MEAN?

THE ART OF MY LIFE
PASSES WITH THE WIND
WHAT DOES IT MEAN?
THE SONGS OF THE BIRDS
SOUNDS OF RUNNING STREAMS
THE SOUND OF LEAVES
WHAT DOES IT MEAN?
THE VOICES OF YESTERDAY
STILL I HEAR
THE PEOPLE, THE MACHINERY
THE MOVEMENT OF LIFE
WHAT DOES IT MEAN?
THE THINGS THAT I HEAR
THE THINGS THAT I HEARD
THE VOICE OF GOD SPEAKING TO ME
WHAT DOES IT MEAN?
YESTERDAY IS GONE
TODAY IS HERE
TOMORROW WILL SOON APPEAR
WHAT DOES IT MEAN?

221)
THE SCRIPTUIRES

I READ THE BIBLE
TO PROTECT MYSELF
FROM ALL THE THINGS
THAT CREATE POOR HEALTH
ALTHOUGH I'M NOT PERFECT
I TRY TO DO WHAT IS RIGHT
I PRAY FOR STRENGTH
EVERYDAY AND EVERY NIGHT
I SEEK FOR THE WISDOM
FOR SOMETHING SOLID TO HOLD
THE WORD IS MY DEFENSE
AGAINST A WORLD SO COLD
IT IS TRULY WRITTEN
THAT THE LIGHT IS THE WAY
TO REPENT OF MY SINS
CONSTANTLY PRAY
SO EVERYDAY I LIVE TRYING
TO BE OBEDIENT AND RIGHT
FOR THE WORD IS MY LIFE
MY EVERLASTILNG LIGHT

222)
THE COMING LIGHT

IF YOU LISTEN CAREFULLY
YOU CAN HERE THE SOUND
OF TRUIMPHETS AND HORNS
THAT VIBRATE THE GROUND
THE SKY WILL SUDDENLY CRACK
A LIGHT WILL APPEAR
ALL THE UNRIGHTEOUS
WILL RUN IN FEAR
A JUDGEMENT WILL BE MADE
THE MOST HOLY COMMAND
A VOICE WILL BE HEARD
THROUGH OUT THE LAND
ALL WILL BE ACCOUNTABLE
BY FAITH OR BY DEED
EVERY KNEE WILL BOW
EVERY RACE, COLOR AND CREED
MADE BY DESIGN
THIS LIGHT WILL APPEAR
AND ALL UNRIGHTEOUS
WILL RUN IN FEAR

223)
THE DENTIST APPOINTMENT

FINALLY THE DAY HAS COME
TO FIX MY WIFES TEETH
THANK GOD FOR NO MORE HEADACHES
NO MORE GRIEF
THEY GAVE HER PENICILLIN
FOR THE PAIN TO SOOTH
THE NEXT APPOINTMENT
SHE'LL COME HOME SMOOTH
BYE, BYE OLD TEETH
THE ROOTS WERE TRASHED
FOR AT LEAST TWO MONTHS
HER FOOD HAD TO BE SMASHED
BUT ON THE NEXT APPOINTMENT
A MIRACLE WILL TAKE PLACE
SOME POP-INS AND POP-OUTS
WILL FILL THE EMPTY SPACE
THANK YOU MR. DENTIST
FOR TAKING AWAY HER PAIN
BECAUSE I WAS WITHIN MOMENTS
OF GOING INSANE
IT FEELS SO MUCH BETTER
TO SEE HER SMILING MORE
SOMETHING THAT SHOULD HAVE BEEN HANDLED A
LONG TIME BEFORE
THIS IS MY WIFE
I LOVE HER NO DOUBT
EVEN IF IT MEANS
FOR THEM ALL TO COME OUT

AS HUSBAND AND WIFE
WE CARRY THE SAME NAME
ALL THE PAIN SHE FEELS
I FEEL THE SAME
THANK YOU GOD
FOR BRINGING HER BACK TO ME
NOW I DON'T NEED MEDICATION
TO KEEP MY SANITY
SHE'S A BEAUTIFUL PERSON
WE WILL ALWAYS BE TOGETHER
THROUGH SICKNESS AND HEALTH
ALL KINDS OF WEATHER
I UNDERSTAND A TOOTH
CAN CAUSE SO MUCH GRIEF
SO THANK YOU MR. DENTIST
FOR THE LOVE OF RELIEF

224)
IRON IN THE FIRE

IT'S ALWAYS GOOD
TO HAVE A BACK UP PLAN
TO DO WHATEVER POSSIBLE
THE BEST THAT YOU CAN
LIFE IS UNPREDICTABLE
SOMETIMES STRANGE
WITH AN IRON IN THE FIRE
YOU CAN MAKE A CHANGE
WITH A COUPLE OF THINGS WORKING
YOU CAN'T GO WRONG
THE SECURITY OF INSURANCE
WILL MAKE YOU STRONG
AN IRON IN THE FIRE
WHEN ONE BURNS OUT
WILL SAVE A PRECIOUS MOMENT
OF BEING IN DOUBT
IN THE SAME FASHION
EVERYDAY YOU MUST PRAY
AN IRON IN THE FIRE
WILL DELIGATE THE WAY

225)
CHANGE

AS THE SUN BEGINS TO SHINE
MY EYES ARE OPEN TO A NEW VIEW
TO WALK THE ROAD OF CHANGE
A ROAD OF VERY FEW
TIME HAS BECOME A FACTOR
CREDITS ARE COUNTED BY THE HOUR
I SEEK EVERY MEANS POSSIBLE
FOR PROSPERITY AND POWER
SO MANY DIFFERENT AVENUES
WHICH ONE CAN I CHOOSE
MY CHOICE WILL DETERMINE
IF I WIN OR LOOSE
SO MUCH I SEE
BY FAITH I FOLLOW MY HEART
UNDER THE HARSHEST SITUATIONS
I TRY TO PLAY THE BEST PART
THE VIEW OF CHANGE IS BEFORE ME
THE PICTURE NEEDS A NEW FRAME
EVERYTHING ELSE IS FADING
IT'S TIME FOR A NEW NAME

226)
PRIORITIES

PRIORITIES ARE THE THINGS
MOST IMPORTANT TO YOU
A CHAIN OF RESPONSIBILITIES
YOU KNOW YOU HAVE TO DO
ORGANIZING THE CATAGORIES
IN WHICH THEY FALL IN PLACE
EACH PRIORITY HAS ITS BOUNDARY
AND A CERTAIN AMOUNT OF SPACE
FOLLOWING YOUR PRIORITIES
IS TO UNDERSTAND YOUR NEEDS
FIND THE BEST FERTILIZER POSSIBLE
AND PLANT YOUR SEEDS
PRIORITIZING CAN WORK
BUT PATIENCE IS A MUST
ALONG WITH RESPECT, SELF DISIPLINE
HONESTY AND TRUST
PRIORITIES CAN SOMETIMES
BRING YOU UP, BRING YOU DOWN
BUT IN THE LONG RUN IT HOLDS
A BRIGHT AND SHINNING CROWN

227)
MY SON

FOR YEARS I PRAYED FOR SOMETHING
THAT I LOST A LONG TIME AGO
HE FINALLY CAME BACK TO ME
WITH THE MOST MAGNIFICENT GLOW
LIKE A REINCARNATION OF ONE BEFORE
HE WAS GIVEN BACK TO ME
ALL THAT I COULD EVER ASK FOR
THE STORY WRITTEN AND MADE TO BE
LIFE HAS A WAY OF GIVING BACK
WITH REALITY, MEASURE, AND REASON
IT HAS A WAY OF BALANCING ITSELF
WITH REFLECTIONS AND SEASON
ANOTHER PART OF LIFE HAS UNFOLDED
A SEED FROM THE SAME BLOOD STREAM
WHAT USE TO BE I HOPE, I WISH
HAS BECOME REALITY, NOT A DREAM
A BEAUTIFUL THING CAME TO LIFE
BY THE POWER OF GODS GRACE
IN THE MIRROR I SEE MYSELF
EVERYTIME I SEE MY SONS FACE

228)
MY WOMAN

YOU BROUGHT SO MUCH JOY
INTO MY LIFE
YOU'RE MY WOMAN, MY QUEEN
MY FOREVER LOVING WIFE
YOU'VE OPENED UP A DOOR
THAT'S BEEN CLOSED FOR MANY YEARS
NOW I'M FILLED WITH HAPPINESS
NO MORE TEARS
I'M NOW DEVOTED TRULY
TO YOUR DEEPEST TOUCH
MY DEDICATION TO YOU
IS TO LOVE YOU MUCH
LIFE OFFERS MANY BLESSINGS
SO PRECIOUS AND DEVINE
I CARRY YOUR LOVE WITH ME
LIKE THE PURENESS OF SWEET WINE
THANK YOU MY LOVE
FOR YOUR BEAUTY IS SO TRUE
FOREVER IN LOVE
DEEPLY WITH YOU

229)
I CAUGHT A WINK

I CAUGHT A WINK FROM THE MOON
AS THE CLOUDS WERE PASSING BY
WHILE SEARCHING FOR GODS FACE
SOMEWHERE IN THE SKY
IT WAS THE PERFECT MOMENT
TO TAKE TIME TO PRAY
AS I WATCHED THE MOON
RUNNING AWAY
A COOL DARK NIGHT
WITH CLOUDS OF GREY
CHASING THE MOON
WHILE IT'S RUNNING AWAY
SHINE ON ME
I PRAY THAT YOU WOULD
TOUCH YOUR FACE
I WISH I COULD
I CAUGHT A WINK FROM THE MOON
AS THE CLOUDS WERE PASSING BY
WHILE SEARCHING FOR GODS FACE
SOMEWHERE IN THE SKY

230)
HEAVEN TIMES SEVEN

IF YOU LOOK DEEP INTO MY EYES
YOU WILL SEE HEAVEN
ALL THAT WE ACCOMPLISH TOGETHER
WILL BE MULTIPLIED BY SEVEN
SOMETHING HAS TO DIE
FOR SOMETHING ELSE TO LIVE
LOVE, PASSION AND RESPECT
IS ALL I HAVE TO GIVE
I JUST WANT TO SEE YOU SMILE
AS WE COME TOGETHER TO PRAY
I WANT US TO LIVE
BEYOND YESTERDAY
NO MATTER WHATEVER FATE
THAT WE MAY FACE
TOGETHER WE CAN OVERCOME ANYTHING
BY THE POWER OF GODS GRACE
EMBRACE THE BEAUTY OF CREATION
FROM THE SPIRIT OF ABOVE
GIVING THE BEST OF ONE ANOTHER
AN UNCONDITIONAL LOVE
IF YOU LOOK DEEP INTO MY EYES
YOU WILL SEE HEAVEN
ALL WE ACCOMPLISH TOGETHER
WILL BE MULTIPLIED BY SEVEN

231)
GODS BUSINESS

WALKING IN FAITH
BEYOND WHAT YOU CAN MEASURE
TO UNDERSTAND SALVATION
A HEAVENLY TREASURE
A GIFT THAT IS GIVEN
ONLY TO BE GIVING BACK
FOR THOSE WHO BELIEVE
THERE IS NO LACK
EMPLOYING THOSE WHO SEEK
ABOVE DARK SITUATIONS
THOSE WHO NO LONGER DESIRE
TO ENTERTAIN TEMPTATION
RECRUITS THE WEAK AND STRONG
WHEN FAITH IS BEING TRIED
YOU MAY BE DELAYED
BUT NOT DENIED
A TRUE WALK UNLEASHES
A TESTIMONY, A WITNESS
A SINNER BECOMES A SAINT
OF GODS BUSINESS

232)
YOU'RE ALL THE INSURANCE I NEED

MY INSURANCE IS PAID IN FULL
FOR THE SAKE OF SIN
TO REDEEM MY SALVATION
SO THAT I CAN LIVE AGAIN
I'M NO LONGER LOST
THE INSURANCE OF DIRECTION
NO MORE FEAR OF THE WORLD
I WEAR THE ARMOUR OF PROTECTION
THE INSURANCE OF THE BLOOD
OVER MY FINANCES
THE INSURANCE OF LIGHT
THROUGH DARK CIRCUMSTANCES
I PLEAD THE BLOOD
OVER SICKNESS AND HEALTH
I HOLD THE INSURANCE
OF SPIRITUAL WEALTH
LOVE, MERCY, FAVOR AND GRACE
IS NOURSIHMENT TO MY SEED
MY LORD JESUS
ALL THE INSURANCE I NEED

233)
A SILENT UNDERSTANDING

I WAS STANDING THERE
WHEN YOU WERE THINKING NEGATIVE OF ME
YOU TRIED TO LOCK ME UP
BUT STILL I WAS FREE
I FELT YOUR ENVY AND JELOUSY
HOPING THAT I WOULD FAIL
I ALSO FELT YOUR ANGER
WHEN YOU SAW ME PREVAIL
TAKING MY KINDESS FOR WEAKNESS
FOR A SELF CENTERED DESIRE
I KNEW I WOULD BE THE ONE YOU WOULD CALL ON
TO PULL YOU OUT OF THE FIRE
WHERE YOU FAIL TO REALIZE
IT DOESN'T MATTER WHAT YOU SAY OR DO
CAUSE THE TRUTH NEEDS NO DEFENDING
IT'S EXPOSING YOU
WE ALL ARE BEING USED

BY THE PURPOSE OF GODS WILL
A SILENT UNDERSTANDING
OF PEACE BE STILL

234)
MORE LIKE ME

I YEARN TO SEE THE MORNINGS
TO MEET THE RISING SUN
MYSELF, THE FATHER AND THE SON
MEETING TOGETHER AS ONE
TO WATCH DARKNESS DISAPPEAR
AS LIGHT CREEPS ACROSS THE GROUND
AND THE MUSIC THAT COMES ALIVE
FROM A VARIETY OF SOUND
THE SILKNESS OF MOISTURE
UPON THE THINGS THAT ARE DRY
AS I WITNESS THE FIRST RAY OF LIGHT
WRITE MY NAME ACROSS THE SKY
SEEING BEYOND MEASURES
I'VE NEVER SEEN BEFORE
ENGAGES A PASSION WITHIN ME
TO WANT TO SERVE YOU MORE
IMAGINING THE PAIN IT TOOK
SO THAT I CAN BE FREE
AS I HEAR THE VOICE OF GOD
SAYING YOU'RE BECOMING
MORE LIKE ME

235)
CHASING YOU

I HAVE CHOSEN TO SPEND
THE REST OF MY LIFE CHASING YOU
THE MOST ULTIMATE FEELING
OF GOING AFTER WHAT IS TRUE
THE TIMES WHEN I WAS BLIND
YOU PASSED ME BY
WHEN I LOST MOTIVATION
AND A DESIRE TO TRY
I RECOGNIZE HOW DARKNESS RAN
WHEN YOU CAME AROUND
I WITNESSED HOW THE EARTH VIBRATES
WHEN YOUR FEET TOUCHED THE GROUND
THE PROCESS OF YOUR HEALING
BY USING LOVE AS A CURE
HOW COULD ANYONE NOT WANT TO CHASE SOMETHING
SO PURE
YOU'VE TAUGHT ME A VALUE
LOVE CAN CARRY ME THROUGH
AS I SPEND THE REST OF MY LIFE
CHASING YOU

236)
HE WILL CARRY YOU THROUGH

WHATEVER YOU'RE GOING THROUGH NOW
THINK BACK ON A TIME OF VICTORY
FROM THE GROUND ROOT OF MEMORIAL, IS MEMORY
SOMETIMES YOU HAVE TO LOOK BACK ON WHAT YOU'VE
ALREADY BEEN THROUGH
SO THAT YOU CAN UNDERSTAND
HOW GOD IS CREATING YOU
IF HE CAN BRING YOU THROUGH
WHAT YOU'VE BEEN THROUGH BEFORE THEN WHAT
MAKES YOU THINK YOU'RE NOT ENTILTED
TO MORE
YOU MAY NEVER BE ABLE
TO REACH AS FAR AS YOU CAN SEE
YOU STILL HAVE THE ABILITY
TO BE ALL YOU CAN BE
SO WHEN YOU FIND YOURSELF STRUGGLING
WITH MORE THAN WHAT YOU FEEL YOU CAN BARE
THINK ABOUT THE LAST BATTLE
THINK ABOUT WHO WAS REALLY THERE

237)
"ASKING VERSES PRAISING"

THE SON THE FATHER THE HOLY SPIRIT
ALL CREATED AS ONE
I THANK YOU FOR ALL THE LOVE
ALL THAT YOU'VE DONE
WITHOUT YOU I CAN NOT BREATH
YOUR BREATH I NEED TO LIVE
THE MORE I THINK ABOUT YOUR LOVE
THE MORE I WANT TO GIVE
SO MUCH THAT I CAN ASK FOR
INSTEAD I GIVE YOU PRAISE
EMBRACE ME AND CARRY ME THROUGH
MY GOOD AND TROUBLED DAYS
AS I CONTINUE TO MOVE FORWARD
MY EYES SEEK YOUR FACE
LOVE, HOPE AND FAITH
KEEPS ME IN MY PLACE
I NEED YOU O'LORD
TO LEAD ME TO THE PROMISE LAND
I NEED YOU O'LORD
TO TAKE ME BY THE HAND

238)
"YOUR" HEART, MY HOME, MY PLACE

WHILE STANDING CLOSE TO YOU
I FELT SOMETHING STRANGE
SOMETHING MYSTERIOUS
SOMETHING WITHOUT RANGE
I WANTED TO SPEAK
I DIDN'T KNOW WHAT TO SAY
SOMETHING MAGICAL WAS MOVING
IN THE MOST BEAUTIFUL WAY
SERIOUSLY IN TOUCH
WITH A DELICATE SITUATION
GOES FAR BEYOND THE THOUGHT
OF JUST INFACTUATION
INSTANTLY FEELING THE NEED
TO EXPLORE THE INSIDE OF YOU
AS I LOOKED UP TO GOD AND ASKED, IS THIS LOVE, IS
THIS TRUE
EVERYTHING DEEP INSIDE OF YOU
PROJECTS A GLOW ON YOUR FACE
TO LIVE INSIDE OF YOUR HEART
CALL IT HOME, MY PLACE

239)
THE HOLIDAYS

A TIME TO COME TOGETHER
ALL DIFFERENCES TO THE SIDE
TO EXPRESS LOVE AND FORGIVENESS, ARMS OPEN WIDE
A MOMENT TO EXCHANGE GIFTS
TO BRING DISTANCE NEAR
TO LAUGH, SHARE MEMORIES
EVEN SHED A TEAR
A HEARTFUL EMBRACE FOR OTHERS
FOR WHO THEY TRULY ARE
BECAUSE DEEP DOWN INSIDE
THERE IS A LIVING STAR
NO MATTER WHAT YOU'VE BEEN THROUGH, OR WHAT
YOU'VE DONE
THE LIGHT BORN UNDER THE STAR
BROUGHT US ALL TOGETHER AS ONE
A TIME TO CHERISH
NEAR OR FAR
BECAUSE DEEP IN EVERY HEART
THERE IS A LIVING STAR

240)
COULD YOU STILL LOVE ME

COULD YOU STILL LOVE ME
IF I BECAME UNEMPLOYED
EVERYTHING THAT WE OWN
SUDDENDLY BECAME VOID
IF I BECAME DISABLED
NOT ABLE TO CARE FOR MYSELF
EVERYTHING THAT USE TO BE HIGH, IS NOW ON THE
BOTTOM SHELF
IF I BECAME PHYSICALLY DEFORMED
NO LONGER APPEALLING TO YOUR EYE, IF I COULD NO
LONGER SEE,
FEEL, TOUCH OR CRY
IF MY FACE WAS TO CHANGE
MY WEIGHT, LOOSE OR GAIN
MENTALLY DISTRUBED, STRESSED
AND IN DEEP EMOTIONAL PAIN
IF I NEEDED YOU BY MY BEDSIDE
COULD YOU STAY
COULD YOU BE THE VOICE THAT I NEED, TO HELP ME PRAY
AMAZINGLY ALL OF THESE THINGS
I CAN'T SEE, THAT'S HOW MUCH LOVING YOU MEANS TO ME

241)
TOUCHED

TOUCHED BY A SOURCE
A SURGE OF SPIRITUAL LIGHT
FEELING A GODLY CONSCIOUS
TO DO ALL THAT I CAN RIGHT
GENERATING A FORCE OF ENERGY
A STRONG WILL TO FIGHT
TO STAND FOR SOMETHING
LIKE A EAGLE, TAKE FLIGHT
A VOLTAGE THAT IS SO HIGH
IT BURNS THROUGH DECEPTION AND FALSE COVERS
SURROUNDS ME WITH A HIGHLIGHT
THAT CAPTIVATES OTHERS
IT OFFERS PURE RESOURCES
OF FAITH, HOPE AND LOVE
WHEN THE WALLS ARE FALLING
IT SEEKS TO LOOK ABOVE
BY A SOURCE OF INSURANCE
THAT NO ONE ELSE COULD GIVE
TOUCHED UNDER THE BLOOD
I WILL ALWAYS LIVE

242)
I NOW SEE

I NOW SEE THE WORLD
WITH TRANSPARENT EYES
NOW ABLE TO SEE THE FALSE
THE DISTORTION, THE LIES
BY THE GIFT OF DISCERNMENT
I CAN SEE BENEATH THE SURFACE
OF BETRAYAL AND MANIPULATION
SELFISH ATTEMPTS OF THOSE WHO
BRING TOXIC COMMUNICATION
I HAVE BEEN BLESSED TO SEE
THE WILL IN THOSE, BUT THEY ARE AFRAID TO TRY
THOSE WHO PRETEND TO BE HAPPY
BEHIND CLOSED DOORS THEY CRY
HOW THE TRUTH IS DISTORTED
FOR SOMETHING WRONG
TO SEEM RIGHT
TEMPTATIONS AND ILLUSIONS
BLINDING THOSE WHO ONCE HAD SIGHT, I CAN SEE WHY
THE TEARS OF GOD CAUSE SO MUCH RAIN
FOR HIS MERCIFUL LOVE HAS BEEN TRADED IN FOR PAIN

243)
WINGS

BORN INNOCENT AND PURE
WITH A BEAUTIFUL SET OF WINGS
TO FLY IS TO LOVE
THE FREEDOM THAT GOD BRINGS
LIFE CAME AS A ECLIPSE
FALLING FAR FROM THE SUN
NO LONGER ABLE TO FLY
I HAVE BROKEN ONE
WEAK BEYOND UNDERSTANDING
CAUGHT IN A WEB OF PERSECUTION
STRUGGLING THROUGH TRIAL,
TEMPTATION AND FALSE SOLUTION
FEAR BECAME A FACTOR
THE REALITY OF NOW BEING THE PRAY, A RESOURCE TO
PREDITORS
CONSEQUENCES OF GOING ASTRAY
GOD LOVES HIS OWN, HIS MERCY AND LOVE HE BRINGS
HE FORGAVE ME OF MY SINS
RESTORED MY WINGS
GIVING ME BACK PEACE
AND THE FREEDOM IT BRINGS
ONLY BY FAITH I EARNED MY WINGS

244)
"YOUR" BLUEPRINT

DEEP BENEATH THE EXTERIOR OF THE FLESH
IS A UNIQUE TREASURE
THAT DEFINES THE PURPOSE OF YOUR LIFE
THAT NO ONE ELSE CAN MEASURE
YOUR DESTINY CAN ONLY BE DETERMINED BY THE
CHOICES YOU MAKE NOT BY THE CHOICES, AND RISKS
THAT OTHER PEOPLE TAKE
WHATEVER FATE YOU MAY FACE
YOUR JOURNEY BELONGS TO YOU
IT'S YOUR GIFT, YOUR BLESSING
FOR NO ONE ELSE TO DO
YOUR LIFE IS ALL YOUR HAVE
BE CAREFUL OF WHO YOU FOLLOW
IT MAY SEEM STRONG ON THE OUTSIDE, BUT ON THE
INSIDE
IT MAY BE HOLLOW
THE HEART SPEAKS THE TRUTH
A PURE VOICE TO LISTEN TO
YOUR BLUEPRINT WAS DESIGNED
AND CREATED FOR ONLY YOU

245)
THE DARK AND THE LIGHT

I VIEW COMMON KNOWLEDGE AS A ATTRIBUTE OF A
GODLY CHARACTERISTIC
WHERE LOVE IS THE ROOT OF TRUTH AND THE FALSE
BECOME REALISTIC
ALL WILL STAND BEFORE JUDGEMENT AND THE TRUTH
WILL BE BALANCED WITH LIES
YOUR LIFE WILL BE PLAYED BACK
BEFORE YOUR VERY EYES
REGARDLESS OF WHAT ANYONE ELSE MAY KNOW
GOD HAS ALREADY COLLECTED THE EVIDENCE
YOUR DECISION TO REPENT OR REMAIN IN DENIAL WILL
DETERMINE YOUR NEXT RESIDENCE
ANYTHING THAT BECOMES A CONVICTION OF AN ACT OF
GUILT DEEP WITHIN
IS TOTALLY AGAINST THE LOVE OF GOD, BUT OF SIN
WHATEVER THE REASON MAY BE
WRONG OR RIGHT
JUDGEMENT WILL FALL UPON
THE DARK AND THE LIGHT

246)
FAIR TO PARTLY CLOUDLY

ON THE OTHER END OF THE PHONE
I CAN HERE THE SOUND OF RAIN
FROM THE TONE OF HER VOICE
I COULD SENSE A FORM OF PAIN
I TRIED A SENSE OF HUMOUR
TO SOMEHOW DRAW OUT A LAUGH
THE RESPONSE I GOT IN RETURN
WAS THAT HER HEART HAD BEEN BROKEN IN HALF
THUNDER STRUCK MY CHEST
IT STARTED TO RAIN ON MY SIDE
SHE IS MY BEST FRIEND
WITH HER I'LL RIDE THE TIDE
UNTIL THE WAVES DIE DOWN
AND THE SUN STARTS TO SHINE
HER FRIENDSHIP PRESERVES MY HEART
LIKE THE FINEST WINE
FAIR TO PARTLY CLOUDLY
A BROKEN HEART TAKES TIME TO MEND, BUT LOVE
STANDS BY
A CLOSE FRIEND

247)
SEE YOU IN HEAVEN
04/24/11

ON THIS SPECIAL DAY
SALVATION CAME TO LIFE
BAPTIZED UNDER THE BLOOD
THE SPIRIT TOUCHED MY WIFE
GLORIFIED BY MAGNIFICENCE
MY PRAYERS HAVE BEEN HEARD
AS I WATCHED THE LOVE OF MY LIFE
SATURATE HERSELF IN THE WORD
SIN HAD TO BE BURRIED
SO THAT PEACE COULD COME ALIVE
THE TEARS OF THE LORD
GIVING REASON TO SURVIVE
ANOTHER SOUL CONVERTED
TO LIVE ON THE TRUE SIDE
TO SECURE THE FOUNDATION
OF WHY CHRIST DIED
MAY OUR CHILDREN CONTINUE TO BE BLESSED
MULTIPLIED BY SEVEN
AS I LOOKED INTO THE EYES OF MY WIFE AND SAID
SEE YOU IN HEAVEN

248)
FROM DARKNESS TO LIGHT

I'VE TURNED MY FACE FROM DARKNESS
TO FACE THE LIGHT
THE FACE OF THE WORLD IS UGLY
BUT THE LORDS FACE IS BRIGHT
LOCKED BEHIND ME ARE
THE DOORS OF MY PAST
THE LAST WILL BE FIRST
AND THE FIRST WILL BE LAST
LOVE, HOPE AND FAITH
I'VE PRAYED FOR THESE
IT'S A BEAUTIFUL THING
TO HAVE MY OWN KEYS
IT'S A BEAUTIFUL THING
TO BE GOING SOMEWHERE
I TRUST IN YOU GOD
TO TAKE ME THERE
EVERYWHERE I GO, EVERYTHING I DO
I KEEP THE LORD IN SIGHT
I'VE TURNED MY FACE FROM DARKNESS
TO FACE THE LIGHT

249)
THE LORD MEDICATES ME

WHEN YOU NEED A PRESCRIPTION
JUST CALL ON ME
NEED I TO REMIND YOU
THAT I'VE BEEN CARRYING THEE
HOWEVER YOU FEEL
REGARDLESS OF YOUR PAIN
I AM THE CURE
TO WIPE AWAY "YOUR" STAIN
NO DOCTOR IN THE WORLD
NO MEDICATION ON EARTH
CAN SAVE YOU MORE THAN I
WHO CREATED YOUR BIRTH
FOR YOUR PAIN IS ONLY AS BAD
AS YOU BELIEVE IT TO BE
I AM THE CURE
IF ONLY YOU BELIEVE IN ME
I AM THE PRESCRIPTION TO YOUR TRIALS, TRIBULATIONS
AND STRIFE
I AM THE BEGINNING AND THE END
THE WAY TO ETERNAL LIFE

250)
THE STAR IN MY EYES

YOU'RE THE STAR IN MY EYES
THAT NO ONE ELSE CAN SEE
A SIGN THAT SAYS
YOU ARE ONLY MEANT FOR ME
IT VIBRATES MY HEART WHEN I THINK
OF THE ATTENTION YOU MUST RECEIVE
YOUR BEAUTY GOES BEYOND SKIN DEEP
SOMETHING INSIDE OF YOU I BELIEVE
A SECRET PLACE INSIDE OF YOU
WHERE NO ONE ELSE HAS BEEN
A PRICELESS REWARD
I WOULD LOVE TO WIN
THE THOUGHT OF MY COMPETITION
FALL FAR FROM MY MIND
WHAT I SEE DEEP INSIDE OF YOU
NO OTHER WOULD SEARCH TO FIND
HOW FAR WOULD I GO
TO WIN SUCH A BEAUTIFUL PRIZE
AS FAR AS THE CLOUDS IN HEAVEN
THE STAR IN MY EYES

251)
TO HOLD ON

TO HOLD ON MEANS TO ENDURE
ALL THAT YOU CAN
IF YOU TRULY LOVE THAT WOMAN
TRULY LOVE THAT MAN
SOMETIMES YOU MAY HAVE TO ACCEPT
LESS THAN WHAT YOU FEEL YOU DESERVE
TO HOLD ON ALSO MEANS
TO SERVE
IT'S SO EASY TO QUIT, TURN YOUR BACK,
TO WALK AWAY
TO HOLD ON MEANS TO BELIEVE
HAVE HOPE, FAITH, AND PRAY
IT MEANS TO OVERCOME OBSTACLES
THAT MAY TRY TO MAKE YOU WEAK
HOLDING ON MEANS
"YOUR" AT THE TOP OF YOUR PEAK
TO HOLD ON MEANS TO ENDURE
ALL THAT YOU CAN
IF YOU TRULY LOVE THAT WOMAN
TRULY LOVE THAT MAN

252)
BEAUTIFUL & BOLD

HOW BEAUTIFUL IS THE SNAKE
AFTER IT SHEDS THE SKIN
THE SAME BEAUTY APPLIES TO YOU
WHEN YOU SHED A LAYER OF SIN
PILES OF ASHES BURN
FROM THE SINS YOU LEAVE BEHIND
FOR THE SAKE OF A NEW LIFE
A DIFFERENT STATE OF MIND
TURNING YOUR BACK ON DARKNESS
ONLY TO FACE THE LIGHT
FOLLOWING THE LORD MAY NOT BE EASY, BUT IT'S
ALWAYS RIGHT
TIME CULTIVATES EVERYTHING
SOMETHINGS ARE MEANT TO SPOIL
BUT THE PURENESS OF GODS LOVE
IS IN THE RICHEST SOIL
EACH LAYER OF SIN THAT IS SHED
ALLOWS THE TRUTH TO UNFOLD
TO REVEAL THE EVIDENCE OF GODS LOVE
OF THE BEAUTIFUL AND BOLD

253)
LIVE TO LEAVE SOMEBODY SOMETHING

I LIKE TO LIVE LONG ENOUGH
TO LEAVE A LEGACY
SOMETHING THAT STANDS FOR TRUTH
NOT A FANTASY
I DON'T WANT TO MAKE HEADLINES
I WANT TO MAKE HISTORY
I WANT TO GO ABOVE AND BEYOND
JUST A MEMORY
I SPEAK LIFE INTO EVERY WORD
FROM THE FLOW OF THIS PEN
FROM THE BEGINNING OF TIME IT WAS WRITTEN THAT I
WAS BORN TO WIN
I REFUSE TO BELIEVE ANYTHING
OTHERWISE
NOT AFTER ALL I'VE BEEN THROUGH
FOR ANYONE READING THIS
THIS MESSAGE IS FOR YOU TOO!
THE MORE YOU SEEK TO SEE THE FACE
OF THE ONE WE SERVE
THE MORE YOU REFUSE TO RECEIVE
ANYTHING LESS THAN WHAT YOU FEEL YOU DESERVE
BECAUSE LOVE SERVES ITSELF
WITH A CONSISTANT OVERFLOW
IT WILL FIND THE DARKEST PLACE
TO PRESENT ITS' GLOW
SOMETHINGS NEED TO BE LIT
IN ORDER TO START A FIRE
THE SAME SOLUTION SHOULD APPLY
TO YOUR HEART, "YOUR" DESTINY
"YOUR" DESIRE

254)
LIVING FOR THE LORD

WHEN YOU'RE LIVING FOR THE LORD
IT MAKES YOU WANT TO BE SOMEBODY
IT WON'T LET YOU LAY BACK
AND BE JUST LODDIE, DODDIE
AT TIMES WE BECOME STUBBORN
DON'T WANT TO FOLLOW THROUGH
THE LORD WILL MAKE IT HIS BUSINESS
TO COME AND GET YOU
WHEATHER YOU WANT TO OR NOT
YOU HAVE BEEN CHOSEN
ALL THE THINGS THAT YOU USE TO DO
SUDDENLY BECOME FROZEN
YOU FIND YOURSELF CONTEMPLATING
WANTING TO DO THINGS RIGHT
CRAVING TO BE AROUND THOSE
WHO GENERATE LIGHT
A GODLY CONSCIOUS SPEAKS
TO LEAD YOU ALONG THE WAY
WITH WISDOM AND KNOWLEDGE
AND NO EXCUSE FOR GOING ASTRAY
THEN YOU BECOME A PROJECTION
OF WHAT IS LIVING DEEP WITHIN
A WITNESS OF THE HOLY SPIRIT
THAT TESTIFIES AGAINST SIN

255)
IN THE GARDEN

ONE MAN, ONE WOMAN
FROM THE SAME BONE
A LONG WITH INSTRUCTIONS
WRITTEN IN STONE
A LAND OF PARADISE
OF BEAUTY AND NO LACK
UNTIL THE VOICE OF MANIPULATION
THREW THE WOMAN OFF TRACK
THE TREE OF GOOD AND EVIL
DO NOT PARTAKE
O'ADAM, O'EVE!!!!
YOU'VE MADE A BIG MISTAKE
YOU'VE PUT ME IN A POSITION
TO SACRAFICE MY SON
AS A WAY OF SALVATION
TO BRING US BACK AS ONE
YOU WILL NO LONGER SEE MY FACE
BECAUSE OF YOUR NEGLECT
THE CAUSE & EFFECT
IS TO DISCONNECT
UNTIL I CAN CLEAN UP THE DAMAGE
OF THIS MESS YOU'VE MADE
ALL THAT YOU TRY TO POSSESS OF THIS WORLD, WILL FADE

256)
HIGH AND LOW

MY TEMPLE IS THE CHURCH
THAT I CAN'T DENY
TO SAY ANYTHING OTHERWISE
I'D BE TELLING A LIE
I JUST ASK FOR THE STRENGTH
TO MAKE ME ABLE
TO KEEP ME FOCUSED
TO KEEP ME STABLE
MY PRIORITIES NEED TO BE IN ORDER
SO THAT I CAN FOLLOW THROUGH
BECAUSE I FIND MYSELF FIGHTING
WITH THINGS I NEED TO DO
IT'S EASIER SAID THEN IT IS DONE
THE THOUGHTS I MAKE
ARE SOMETIMES DIFFERENT
THEN THE ACTIONS I TAKE
SOMETIMES I WONDER
AM I GOING TO GET THERE
I DON'T WANT TO SPEND MY WHOLE LIFE, JUST
WONDERING WHERE
THE FEAR OF BEING IN VIOLATION
OF NO CALL, NO SHOW
THE FEAR OF LOOSING FOUNDATION
HIGH AND LOW

257)
THE WHITE DOVE

IT'S EARLY IN THE MORNING
CLOUDS PASS BY THE MOON
IN ANOTHER DIRECTION IS A LIGHT
OF THE SUN COMING UP SOON
THANKFUL FOR THE BREATH OF LIFE
TO CATCH GOD IN ACTION
THE NURTURING OF HIS CREATION
IS A BEAUTIFUL ATTRACTION
AS A LITE MIST OF FOG
DIMINISHES UPON THE EARTH
I CAN FEEL THE SPIRIT OF THE LORD
ONCE AGAIN GIVING BIRTH
TO SEE IT, HEAR IT AND FEEL IT
BRINGS PEACE TO MY SOUL
MY FAITH AND DEPENDENCE ON HIM
IS MY ULTIMATE GOAL
WHATEVER I MAY FACE TODAY
EVERYTHING IS GOING TO BE ALRIGHT
BECAUSE I WALK IN LOVE
WITH THE COMPANY OF LIGHT
IN DEEP EMBRACEMENT
MY HEART OVERFLOWS WITH LOVE
AS THE SPIRIT LANDS ON MY SHOULDERS, THE WHITE DOVE

258)
LIFELESS WITHOUT YOU

I CAN'T IMAGINE
LIVING WITHOUT YOU
WHERE WOULD I GO?
WHAT WOULD I DO?
THE THOUGHT OF BEING ALONE
GIVES ME A SENSE OF FEAR
A DRIED UP SOUL
WITHOUT A SINGLE TEAR
I CAN'T SEE MYSELF
WITHOUT SECURITY OR PROTECTION
"YOUR" WISDOM, YOUR KNOWLEDGE,
"YOUR" LOVE, YOUR DIRECTION
WITHOUT YOUR BLOOD
MY VAINS MAY AS WELL BE FILLED WITH DUST
WHERE DARKNESS FINDS A HOME
IN A HEART DECAYING OF RUST
LIVING WITHOUT YOU
JUST DOESN'T SEEM RIGHT
I CAN'T IMAGINE WALKING THROUGH LIFE, WITHOUT LIGHT

259)
TEACH ME LORD

TEACH ME HOW TO BE LIKE YOU
HOW TO LOVE LIKE YOU DO
ABOUT DISCERNMENT
OF THE FALSE, THE TRUE
TEACH ME HOW TO ACCEPT FAILURE
AS WELL AS SUCCESS
HOW TO APPRECIATE PLENTY
HOW TO BE THANKFUL FOR LESS
TEACH ME ABOUT PATIENCE
HOW TO CRAWL BEFORE I WALK
HOW TO LISTEN TO WHAT I WANT TO SAY BEFORE I TALK
TEACH ME HOW TO BE
A RESOURCE TO ANOTHER
TEACH ME HOW TO FISH
FOR MY SISTERS, MY BROTHERS
TEACH ME IN A WAY
I'VE NEVER BEEN TAUGHT BEFORE
ABOUT ETERNAL LIFE
AND LOVE FOREVER MORE

260)
THE RIGHT BAIT

THE LARGEST FISH I EVER CAUGHT
WAS AT THE BOTTOM OF THE LAKE
'IT' FAUGHT AS IF IT KNEW
THAT IT'S LIFE WAS AT STAKE
SOME OF THE MOST POWERFUL THINGS
COME FROM LOW PLACES
SOME OF THE MOST BEAUTIFUL SMILES
COME FROM SAD FACES
CHANGE IS SOMETIMES HARD TO ACCEPT
ESPECIALLY WHEN YOU'VE BEEN THROUGH SO MUCH
THE REALITY OF ANYTHING DIFFERENT
IS COMPLETELY OUT OF TOUCH
THE GREATEST CHALLENGE IN LIFE
A FIGHT TO ADAPT A CHANGE
ANYTHING THAT IS NOT FAMILIAR
MEANS EVERYTHING IS STRANGE
CERTAIN THINGS WILL FOLLOW
DEPENDING ON HOW THEY'RE BEING LED
CERTAIN THINGS WILL LOOSE AN APPETITE BECAUSE OF
WHAT THEY'RE BEING FED
ALTHOUGH IT MAY BE A STRUGGLE
TO HAVE THE PATIENCE TO WAIT
WHEN FISHING FOR A MAN
IT TAKES THE RIGHT BAIT

261)
A FALSE LOVE

LIKE A SNAKE IT WAITS
FOR THE RIGHT TIME TO STRIKE
IT SMILES IN YOUR FACE
WHILE PORTRAYING ACTS OF DISLIKE
A MANIPULATING TONE PRETENDING TO LOVE WITH A
HIDDEN AGENDA
ON THE DOWN LOW
A SELFISH LONG GAME
WHILE DRAINING YOU SLOW
WITH NO REMORSE OR APPRECIATION
AFTER EVERYTHING IS SAID AND DONE
IT TURNS THE PROBLEM FROM ITSELF
AND MAKES LIKE YOU'RE THE ONE
A NON-SHALON ATTITUDE
THAT WILL CLAIM NOT TO KNOW
ANYTHING THAT IT DOES
AND WILL HAVE THE NERVE TO SOMETIMES," SAY SO"
SELF CENTERED AND DESPERATE
PROCALIMING A SPIRITUAL WALK
IT JUSTIFIES ITS ACTIONS
WITH A LOT OF GODLY TALK
IT WILL EVEN INVEST ITSELF
FOR CONFIDENCE TO HAVE ITS TURN
IN THE FURNACE OF ITS DESIRE
IT'S YOU IT SEEKS TO BURN
OFFERING ITSELF TO DO FAVORS
PROVIDING FOR MANY THINGS
BUT BEHIND CLOSED DOORS

A LITTLE BIRD SINGS
IT STALKS WITH THE FULL INTENTION
USING FALSE LOVE AS LEVERAGE
TAKING KINDNESS FOR WEAKNESS
AND BLOOD AS ITS BEVERAGE
IT WILL PRETEND TO BE YOUR PARTNER
YOUR MOON, YOUR SUN
A FALSE LOVE IS WORSE
THAN A LOADED GUN

THE GENTLEMAN

IT'S BROKEN DOWN INTO TWO WORDS
GENTLE-MAN
HE IS ONE WHO ACKNOWLEDGES GOD AT ALL TIMES
BECAUSE TO BE AWARE IS TO BE ALIVE. HE HAS AN
AUTOMATIC SENSE OF MAKING ONES AROUND HIM FEEL
COMFORTABLE AND WILL NEVER LEAD ANOTHER IN A
DIRECTION HE WOULDN'T GO HIIMSELF.
WITH A STRONG BRIDGE OF COMMUNICATION
HE EXERCISES A DEEP MEANS OF RESPECT AND
APPRECIATION AND HIS MIND AND HEART IS BUILT ON
UNDERSTANDING AND COMPROMISING ON THE THINGS
WITHIN REASON.
HE IS AWARE OF THE SMALL THINGS THAT ARE AT
TIMES OVER LOOKED AND CARRIES A POSITIVE AND
PRODUCTIVE NATURE THAT TAKES FULL RESPONSIBILITY
AND AUTHORITY FOR ALL HE CREATES RIGHT OR WRONG
BECAUSE HE KNOWS HE IS NOT PERFECT AND THE ONLY
THING THAT CAN AFFECT HIM ARE THE THINGS HE ALLOWS.
HE DOESN'T WORRY ABOUT THE THINGS HE CAN'T
CONTROL AND HE SHINES WITH A DEEP SENSE OF
SECURITY, HUMBLENESS AND IS CONTENT WITH A
DEEP BELIEF AND A FAITH THAT SHOWS THROUGH HIS
ACTIONS.
HE IS NOT JUDGEMENTAL NOR DOES HE HOLD RECORD
OF WRONG AND MONEY, MATERIAL WEALTH AND
FLESHLY DESIRES ARE NOT AN ISSUE.

A GENTLE-MAN REALIZES THAT WHAT LIVES INSIDE OF
HIM IS WORTH MORE THAN ANYTHING THIS WORLD
HAS TO OFFER SO THEREFORE ALL OTHER THINGS WILL
EVENTUALLY MANIFEST ITSELF.

PEACE

*A FORCE THAT SURPASSES ALL UNDERSTANDING AND
THE MOMENT THAT YOU HAVE FULLY ACCEPTED PEACE
IN YOUR HEART YOU INSTANTLY POSSESS A POWER OF
AND UNMOVABLE FORCE. A FORCE THAT AT TIMES
WILL DEMONSTRATES ITSELF IN THE SIGN, AND IN THE
SERVICE OF LOVE.*
*IT SHOWS THAT ITS TALK IS IN LINE WITH ITS WALK. IT'S
THE KIND OF PEACE THAT ONE CAN FIND SELF-COMFORT
REGARDLESS OF THE SITUATIONS, CONDITIONS,
CIRCUMSTANCES, OR WHATEVER THE STATUS MAY BE.
IT DOESN'T ALLOW ITSELF TO BE DISTURBED BY
UNHEALTHY ISSUES AND WILL NOT PLAY A PART IN TOXIC
COMMUNICATION. THE PEACE THAT I KNOW SAYS THAT
I CAN RISE ABOVE EVERYTHING THAT CRITICIZES MY
CHARACTER AND MY PERSONALITY.*
*IT DOESN'T SEE ITSELF TO BE ABOVE OTHERS, BUT YET
IT SAYS I LOVE YOU EVEN IF YOU MAY HATE ME AND IT
DOESN'T LOWER ITSELF TO BE SEDUCED BY THE SINFUL
NATURE OF THE FLESH BECAUSE IT UNDERSTANDS THE
NATURE OF SIN.*

*MAY GOD CONTINUE TO KEEP YOU ALL UNDER HIS
UMBRELLA OF PEACE AND BLESSINGS*

MAY CREATIVE MINDS COME TOGETHER

EDWARD E. MCGILL

INDEX

CPSIA information can be obtained
at www.ICGtesting.com
Printed in the USA
FFOW02n1410131015
17662FF

9 781466 907720